FAMOUS
BLACK
AMERICANS

by John T. King and Marcet H. King
illustrations by Don Collins and Gary McElhaney

STECK-VAUGHN
C O M P A N Y
Elementary • Secondary • Adult • Library

ABOUT THE AUTHORS

Dr. John T. King, president of Huston-Tillotson College and a distinguished black educator, received his B.A. degree from Fisk University and his B.S. degree from Huston-Tillotson College. He earned his M.S. degree from DePaul University and his Ph.D. from the University of Texas at Austin. With over twenty-eight years of experience as a college teacher and administrator, Dr. King has written many articles for professional and religious journals and is a coauthor of several mathematics textbooks.

Mrs. Marcet H. King, wife of Dr. King and an effective teacher with almost two decades of classroom experience, received her B.A. degree from Fisk University and her Master of Music degree from the Chicago Musical College. She has taught in the public schools in Austin and Chicago and on the college level at Huston-Tillotson College.

Consultant
Shirley A. Smith
Teacher–Trainer Consultant
Social Studies Enhancement
Holland School
Dorchester, Massachusetts

Cover Design
Lee R. Castro

Copyright © 1995 By Steck-Vaughn Publishing Corporation, Austin, Texas
ISBN 0-8114-4324-8
    5 6 7 8 9 0 DBH 99 98 97 96

PREFACE

The United States of America is often called "the melting pot of the world" because of the many different races, backgrounds, and cultures represented here. People from every foreign country have come to the United States, have made this land their home, and have worked to make this nation a good place to live. Many of these people have achieved personal fame and success for their contributions to society.

This book was written to relate some of the worthwhile contributions that have been made by black Americans—achievements in science, medicine, education, politics, athletics, music, industry, and other fields of human activity.

In addition to recording some of the accomplishments of black Americans, this book provides biographical sketches of black men and women who proved that fame and success can result from personal drive and honest efforts.

The authors' straightforward, factual account of the lives of these famous Americans shows that in America the achievements of the individual are recognized. Through their actions these men and women have earned honor for themselves and their country.

CONTENTS

Richard Allen

PREACHER

There are many kinds of pioneers. A person who is first to enter or settle a region is called a pioneer. Those who are first to open or prepare a way for others to follow are also called pioneers. Richard Allen was a pioneer in the field of religion. He became the first black bishop in America.

Richard Allen was born in 1760 near Philadelphia, Pennsylvania. Like most black Americans born at that time, Richard Allen was a slave. He was more fortunate than many slaves, though. He had a kind master who did not believe in separating slave families. When Richard was a small boy, his family was together.

Richard's master was Benjamin Chew, a Quaker. He was more than a master to the Allen family. He was a friend. He believed in educating his slaves so that they could improve themselves.

Even when Richard was a small child, he wanted to preach. He would often go off by himself and talk for hours. Young Richard knew that he had to practice to become a good preacher.

Since Benjamin Chew was an impor-tant man, many people came to his home. Richard was able to see them and hear them talk. Mr. Chew always managed to give Richard a job to do in the room where the men were. That way he could listen to the conversations. He felt that Richard could learn just by listening to others talk.

Although Mr. Chew was a good man, he was a poor businessman. His debts became so great that he had to sell some of his slaves. He did not want to separate the mother from her children, so he sold the entire Allen family. Richard was seven at that time.

For a while the Allen family was happy in the new surroundings. However, the new master was not able to feed all his slaves, and he sold Richard's mother and the younger children. He kept Richard and one brother.

Richard's mother often had talked to her children about freedom. She had told them how she and her mother had been mistreated. When she was separated from Richard and his brother, she urged them to work hard and save their money. She wanted them to buy their freedom some day.

When Richard grew a little older, he began to attend prayer meetings. His master let the boys attend these meetings and also hold religious services on the farm. At that time, many other slave owners did not allow their slaves to do this.

When Richard had learned to read and write, he became a leader in the Methodist Society. He met many important Methodist leaders, and his master allowed him to invite some of them to the house. As a result of these visits, his master became a Christian.

Some slaves were permitted to earn money for themselves. Richard's master offered him and his brother their freedom for two thousand dollars. He let them earn money in various ways. This made the boys happy, for they wanted to be free. Slavery was hard, even under a kind master.

The Revolutionary War was going on at that time. Richard got a job as a wagon driver. He worked very hard and saved his money. Finally he had saved the two thousand dollars. He bought freedom for himself and his brother.

As soon as he was free, Richard Allen became a traveling preacher. There were very few black preachers in 1783, although there were a few blacks who went as helpers for white preachers. Harry Hosier, called "Black Harry," was such a helper for the great Francis Asbury. Hosier was a lively preacher whose sermons were enjoyed by whites and blacks alike. Allen and Hosier became friends. It was through "Black Harry" that Allen met Francis Asbury and Dr. Thomas Coke, early Methodist leaders.

Though Richard Allen had been born in slavery and had received very little education, he had learned many useful lessons. He had discovered that a free black person found it hard to make a living. He felt that blacks needed to learn trades. He began to study how to make shoes.

While Allen was learning the trade of shoemaking, he was called to Philadelphia. A black preacher was needed to teach blacks in the city. Allen was asked to serve as a helper at St. George Methodist Church. The church building had just been bought by the Methodists and was to be for blacks as well as whites. Since it needed repairing very badly, Richard Allen organized the black people into groups and directed them in repairing the church. When it was finished, they collected money to help furnish it. This was the first real church that many of them had ever had. They were very proud of their church.

Soon many people of both races began to attend services at St. George Church. As the crowd grew larger, there was a disagreement about seating arrangements. To avoid further trouble, Richard Allen led all the blacks out of the church. He organized a separate congregation—Bethel Church. Absalom Jones, another black preacher, helped him through these troublesome times.

In 1793 a great epidemic of yellow fever spread in Philadelphia. There were not enough doctors and nurses. The dead were often left unburied. It was thought that blacks could not catch the fever since few of them died from it.

Again Richard Allen was called upon to organize a committee of black people. This was another worthy cause—saving the lives of others. He and his friend Absalom Jones were taught how to care for the sick. They trained other blacks and worked day and night. Blacks tended the sick and buried the dead. After the epidemic was over, Richard Allen's fame as a minister and civic leader spread.

In 1794 Allen began to organize

churches in other cities. He worked hard in his shoe shop to earn money for his work. His business grew, and he hired people to work with him. This gave Allen more time to work with his church.

Because of Allen's good work, Bishop Asbury ordained him as a deacon in 1799. He continued to be a leader in the church and to organize new churches. In 1816 he organized the African Meth-odist Episcopal Church, an all-black denomination. At that time he was elected and consecrated as a bishop.

The denomination which Bishop Allen founded has over a million members to-day. It owns hundreds of beautiful churches and is now supporting several good colleges. Although Bishop Allen died on March 26, 1831, his name has been kept alive through his good works.

Understanding the Story

Match the beginning part of each sentence in Column A with its ending in Column B. Write the correct letter of the ending on the blank before each beginning in Column A.

Column A

1. _____ Richard Allen was born

2. _____ Richard was separated

3. _____ Richard's first master was

4. _____ Richard Allen became

5. _____ Allen got a job and bought

6. _____ Richard learned the trade

7. _____ Allen served as a helper

8. _____ During an epidemic of yellow fever,

9. _____ Richard Allen was elected a bishop at the time

10. _____ Bishop Allen died

11. _____ In 1793 there was

12. _____ When Richard was a small child,

Column B

a. freedom for himself and his brother.

b. on March 26, 1831.

c. a traveling preacher.

d. in 1760 near Philadelphia.

e. Allen cared for the sick.

f. Benjamin Chew.

g. of shoemaking.

h. he organized the African Methodist Episcopal Church.

i. from his mother and the younger family members.

j. at St. George Methodist Church.

k. he wanted to preach.

l. a great epidemic of yellow fever in Philadelphia.

Finding Synonyms

Synonyms are words that have the same or almost the same meanings. Choose the correct synonym and write it in the blank following each word.

area   better   complete   find   unfolded

lucky   liability   purchase   helpful   shun

1. discover   _____

2. improve   _____

3. spread   _____

4. entire   _____

5. avoid   _____

6. fortunate   _____

7. useful   _____

8. debt   _____

9. region   _____

10. buy   _____

Louis Armstrong

MUSICIAN

No other place could have been more fitting as the birthplace of Louis Armstrong than the colorful city of New Orleans. It is a merry and lively city. The people there enjoy their colorful city, and they are proud of Louis Armstrong.

Louis Armstrong was a happy and easy-going person who made friends all over the world. July 4, 1900, seems a perfect day for the birth of one so free and independent. But being born in James Alley was a poor beginning for Louis. His family was poor. His father was not home very much and later deserted the Armstrong family. Louis's mother had to work all day to support her family. Her work meant leaving Louis and his sister, Beatrice, alone most of the time.

For a while Louis did very well without the watchful eye of his mother. His love for music helped to keep him busy. He gathered four of his young friends together and formed a little musical band. They were ragged little children and a sad sight to see. But they were smart youngsters, and they made their own musical instruments. They started playing on the street corners for pennies.

Louis and his friends made others happy with their music. To reward the children for the music, people often pitched pennies to them. Because his pockets were ragged, Louis had no place to put his pennies. He didn't want to lose them, so he put them in his mouth. Louis's mouth was very big and could hold quite a few pennies. Before long everyone began calling him "Satchelmouth." Later "Satchelmouth" became "Satchmo."

As a little boy Louis sold papers at a newsstand on Canal Street, one of the busiest streets in New Orleans. He always had a bright smile for everyone. His voice could be heard loud and clear above the noise of heavy traffic. Since he had a deep, rough voice, the people for blocks around could hear him when he sang or yelled, "Paper, paper!"

When Louis wasn't working, he wandered about the streets of New Orleans. Wherever there was music, he found it. The custom in New Orleans in those days was for marching bands to play at picnics, carnivals, and funerals. When there was a funeral, Louis and other boys and girls would follow the bands to the cemetery. On the way back the children would dance beside the bands in the dusty streets. Happy music was always played coming back from the cemetery. This happy music was jazz in the making.

One New Year's Eve Louis was having fun with some friends. Several other people were celebrating by shooting at bottles with their pistols. Louis had never fired a gun before, but he thought it would be fun. He didn't know it was against the law to fire a gun in the city, so he shot at the bottles. When the policemen came, Louis's friends ran. But it was too late for Louis. Many of the other people had been disturbing the neighborhood for a long time before that night. When the policemen found Louis, they took him to jail. They believed that he was bad and sent him to the Waif's Home for Boys.

At first Louis was very unhappy at the Home. The boys were not friendly. He missed his mother and his sister. He also missed his favorite meal of red beans and rice. He was no longer free to roam the streets and to dance to the music of the marching bands. But his unhappiness did not last very long. The happy music of the Waif's Band began to interest him.

Louis listened every day while the Waif's Band practiced. He hoped Mr. Peter Davis, the teacher, would ask him to join the band. Louis wanted to blow the golden cornet just like "Papa Joe" Oliver, the great musician from New Orleans.

One day Mr. Davis did ask him to join the band. Instead of a cornet, Louis was given a tambourine. This did not bother Louis. He wanted to be a part of the band and would play any instrument. Soon he was moved to the drums. Keeping a good

beat seemed to come naturally to him.

Louis soon got the chance he was waiting for. The boy who blew the bugle was taken home by his parents. Louis asked Mr. Davis to let him take the boy's place. He promised to practice hard so that he could blow reveille, taps, and mess call. Mr. Davis knew how Louis felt, so he gave him the job and told him to practice. Louis was so happy that he worked all night polishing his bugle. The next morning the dirty green horn that Mr. Davis had given Louis was shiny brass. The other boys cheered Louis when they saw the shiny bugle.

Life at the Home changed when Louis became the bugler. Waking up to beautiful sounds in the morning was a joy. Everyone enjoyed his soft, clear tones. Playing the bugle came easily to Louis.

Within a few weeks Mr. Davis gave Louis a cornet. Now Louis was really happy. Now he could learn to play like "Papa Joe."

The Waif's Band soon became very popular. And Louis had learned to play so well that he became the leader of the band. The band played at picnics and social clubs. The band was asked to march in parades. Louis was always up front, leading the band with the sweet notes of the cornet. How proud and excited he was when he marched in his old neighborhood! His friends were very proud, too. They crowded the sidewalks and tossed him money. The money would help pay for new band uniforms.

When Louis had served his time at the Waif's Home, he returned to his family. He was fourteen and very mature for his age, but he cried when he left the Home. He didn't want to leave his horn and the band behind.

Once out of the Home, Louis began to look for a job. Jazz musicians were needed, but the pay was not good. Louis needed to make money for his family, and he found two jobs. During the day he delivered coal in a cart that was pulled by a mule. In the evening he played with a band at one of the local night spots.

Louis Armstrong didn't have enough money to buy a horn, but the owner of the place bought one for him at a pawn shop. Getting the horn and the job marked the beginning of a long and successful career in jazz. He started out working for fifty cents a night. Later in his career, Louis Armstrong was paid large sums for one night's work.

One of the remarkable things about Louis Armstrong was his great ability to understand and feel the music that people loved to hear. Although he could not read notes very well, he had a good ear. Once he heard a tune, he could play it on his trumpet. He learned to play almost every kind of music. But he especially liked to play blues, ragtime, jazz, spirituals, and funeral marches.

One night, because of a sore lip, Louis Armstrong sang his trumpet part instead of playing it. Members of his band liked it. His "sandpaper" voice was funny, and the customers liked it. The singing became a part of his act even after his lip had healed.

After his show became popular in New Orleans, Louis Armstrong began to travel. He went from New Orleans to St. Louis and Chicago. He played in New York and Los Angeles. He played with every great band and jazz musician in the United States. His name was known everywhere.

Louis Armstrong became known as America's "Ambassador of Jazz." People in countries all over the world looked forward to his concerts. He knew that his music could help other nations have more respect for the United States. By providing good music that people enjoyed, Louis Armstrong helped people to understand and respect each other, with no regard to race or color.

Louis Amstrong said that to be a success every musician had to keep his own style. He had to be original and not imitate others. And he said that if a person remembered to smile and tried to get along with others, he could be successful, no matter who the person was.

Louis "Satchmo" Armstrong was a poor child from a back alley of New Orleans. But he knew what he wanted to do in life, and he worked hard to reach his goals. He was a great person and a great American.

Reviewing the Story

Fill in each blank with the word or words which completes each sentence correctly.

1. Louis Armstrong was born in the city of _____.

2. As a child, Louis received pennies for playing music on street corners, and kept

   the pennies in his _____.

3. When Louis first played with the Waif's Band, the instrument he was given to play

   was a _____.

4. Soon Louis was given the _____ to play, and he blew it

   every morning.

5. When Louis was given a _____, he wanted to learn to play it like "Papa Joe" Oliver.

6. At the age of fourteen, Louis left the _____ and returned to his family.

7. While living with his family, Louis worked during the day, and he _____ _____ at night.

8. When Louis Armstrong first played with a band at a night spot, he earned _____ _____ a night.

9. Since people all over the world enjoyed Louis Armstrong's music, he was known as America's "_____."

10. Louis Armstrong was always original in the way he performed his music, and he would never _____ other musicians.

Finding Antonyms

Antonyms are words that have opposite meanings. Choose the correct antonym and write it in the blank following each word.

inactive	artificial	catch	failure
drab	follower	smooth	earlier

1. natural _____

2. colorful _____

3. rough _____

4. later _____

5. success _____

6. lively _____

7. leader _____

8. toss _____

Benjamin Banneker

INVENTOR AND
MAN OF PEACE

Many people laughed in 1761 when they heard of the black man who studied the stars at night. "What a strange man! Who ever heard of a black scientist!" they said. "He must be out of his mind. A black person can't learn!"

But Benjamin Banneker did learn. He became an astronomer, mathematician, poet, clockmaker, surveyor, and crusader for freedom. By the time he was sixty, he was probably the best-known black person in America. Many of the people who had made fun of him began to praise him. When he rode through the streets of his hometown near Baltimore, people often surrounded him just to look at him and to hear him speak. They wanted to hear about the famous people he had met. They wanted to hear of his travels. This heavily built, gray-haired man usually wore a fine broadcloth long coat and a wide-brimmed hat. He was quite a sight to see and a pleasure to listen to.

Banneker was a restless person who always wanted to learn. He was interested in everything around him. The sky and all of nature attracted him. There was so much that he felt he could learn by just watching the wonders of the world.

Benjamin Banneker was born near Baltimore, Maryland, in 1731. He was born free and had many things that most blacks at that time did not have. He had a comfortable home and a chance to go to a private school for both white and black children. He began to read more and more. He couldn't find enough books to keep him busy.

One day Benjamin Banneker had to drop out of school. He was needed at home to help his father with the farm chores. Having to leave school made little Benjamin very unhappy. Taking care of cows and helping with the planting took too much time away from his reading. He did not like being a farmer's son. Farm work bored him.

Not being able to go to school did not keep Banneker from learning all he could. He improved his reading and writing skills. He began to teach himself. He had a scientific mind, and he did simple experiments with homemade equipment.

Everything around him became his private school.

Working on the farm did have some advantages. Banneker learned to use his hands. With a borrowed watch as a model, Banneker built the first wooden clock ever made in America. All of the parts of the clock were carved out of wood. In later years, many people came from miles around just to see his strange clock.

When Banneker's father and mother died, the farm became his responsibility. Most young people in those days would have considered owning land something to be happy about, but not Banneker. He felt that the farm would take too much of his time. He would not be able to study as he had in the past.

Good luck came into Banneker's life when George Ellicott and his family moved into the neighborhood. This Quaker family came to open a flour mill. When George Ellicott met Banneker, he was surprised at the many things that this quiet black man knew and could do. He wanted to help Banneker. Mr. Ellicott's sons were astronomers and mathematicians, and they gave Banneker scientific books and instruments that he could use to study the heavens.

Since the farm was such a burden, Banneker turned the farm over to his new friends, the Ellicotts. He was paid every year for the use of his land. This freed him from having to take care of the farm, and it gave him more time to study.

Benjamin Banneker never married. After his parents died, he lived alone in a log cabin. Many people called him odd because of the way he lived. He studied at night, slept in the morning, and worked in the afternoon. Banneker washed his own clothes, took care of a small garden, and cooked his own meals.

Many times at night Banneker would wrap himself in a heavy cloak and lie under a tree. He often stayed there all night looking at the stars and studying the heavens. With the books and instruments that he had received from the Ellicotts, he made an excellent prediction of an eclipse of the sun. Two years later, in 1791, he published his first almanac, which had a calendar for the year. The almanac gave facts about the weather and other useful information.

Banneker also studied mathematics. He often wrote to other mathematicians with questions about difficult problems. The table in his house was always covered with books and papers. He never seemed to rest. He was greedy about learning more and more.

As Banneker's name became known in America, many famous people wanted to meet him. These people did not think of his color; they respected the power of his mind. Our first president, George Washington, asked Banneker to help lay out the territory which later became Washington, D. C. Banneker became the first black person to receive a presidential appointment. He and two other people planned where streets and buildings would be built in the new city.

Banneker realized that many other people were not as fortunate as he. He always was ready to share his home and his knowledge with anyone in need. He defended the rights of his people, and he was not afraid to speak about the things that he did not like.

Benjamin Banneker was also a man of peace. He said that our government needed a Secretary of Peace, who would work for world peace with other nations. In 1793 he wrote a plan for peace. Over a hundred years later President Woodrow Wilson had a similar idea—the League of Nations.

Banneker once said, "Parades and uniforms attract young men. They should be done away with. Were there no uniforms, there would probably be no armies."

In addition to wanting world peace, Banneker wanted every person to be free. He felt that every person in the United States should have the opportunity to work and to live as a free American. He believed that every man, woman, and child should enjoy the freedom that the great Americans had in mind when they wrote our Declaration of Independence. He believed that every person should have the right to "...life, liberty, and the pursuit of happiness."

Benjamin Banneker died in 1806 at the age of seventy-five. Just before he died, a fire destroyed some of his writings. However, most of his writings and copies of his almanac are in the Library of Congress in Washington, D.C.

Finding the Meanings

Match each word in Column A with its meaning in Column B. Write the correct letter of the meaning on the blank before each word in Column A.

Column A	Column B
1. _____scientist	a. to cut off or obscure the light from
2. _____experiment	b. having good luck
3. _____equipment	c. the act of telling beforehand
4. _____astronomer	d. a person who is trained in science
5. _____eclipse	e. furnishings or supplies
6. _____almanac	f. performing trials or tests to find out something
7. _____fortunate	g. a person who studies the sun, moon, and other heavenly bodies
8. _____prediction	h. a calendar that also gives other valuable information

Understanding the Story

Write true or false before each of the following statements.

1. _____Benjamin Banneker became an astronomer and a poet.

2. _____Banneker was born near Cleveland, Ohio.

3. _____George Ellicott was a good friend to Banneker and wanted to help him.

4. _____Banneker was not interested in studying mathematics.

5. _____Benjamin Banneker helped lay out the territory which later became Washington, D.C.

6. _____In 1803 Banneker wrote a plan for peace.

Reviewing the Story

Underline the word or group of words which completes each sentence correctly.

1. When Benjamin Banneker was young, he and his family lived   **(a) in a city**   **(b) on a farm**   **(c) on a ranch** .

2. When Benjamin had to drop out of school, he   **(a) began teaching himself**   **(b) hired a tutor**   **(c) lost interest in his studies** .

3. Banneker was born in the year   **(a) 1813**   **(b) 1792**   **(c) 1731** .

4. Banneker usually worked   **(a) in the afternoon**   **(b) at night**   **(c) in the morning** .

5. In 1793 Banneker   **(a) published his first almanac**   **(b) built the first wooden clock**   **(c) wrote a plan for peace** .

6. Most of Benjamin Banneker's writings are kept in the   **(a) White House**   **(b) Library of Congress**   **(c) Smithsonian Institute** .

Mary McLeod Bethune

EDUCATOR

Four United States presidents—Coolidge, Hoover, Roosevelt, Truman—appointed Mary McLeod Bethune to government posts. In 1936 President Franklin D. Roosevelt appointed her director of a special division of the National Youth Administration. She became the first black woman to head a federal agency. President Roosevelt valued her wisdom and insight and often called upon her while he served as president. She became a familiar figure at the White House during Roosevelt's terms as president.

Mary Jane McLeod was born in 1875 in South Carolina. She was the first free child to be born in her parent's home. Her older brothers and sisters had been born slaves. After the Civil War, Mary's mother worked for her former master until the family had money to buy five acres of land from him. The family built a cabin on the land, and the children worked in the rice and cotton fields. At the age of nine, Mary McLeod could pick 250 pounds of cotton a day but could not read.

While Mary McLeod was nine years old, the first free school was started in the neighborhood by Emma Wilson, a black missionary. Mary McLeod walked five miles each way to school and then in the evenings taught her family what she had learned. By the age of fifteen, she had taken every subject offered at the school. Because of family financial problems, Mary McLeod knew that higher education would not be possible for her.

Then, a dressmaker in Denver, Colorado, heard about Emma Wilson's school. The dressmaker offered to pay for the higher education of one needy student from the school. Mary McLeod was selected, and she went to Scotia Seminary in Concord, North Carolina. She was very happy during the years she spent there.

After leaving Scotia Seminary, Mary McLeod decided that she wanted to help others. She wanted to be a missionary. She had a scholarship to Moody Bible Institute in Chicago and completed her courses in 1895. Mary McLeod offered to do missionary work in Africa, but she was told that there were no openings. Instead, she worked as an assistant to Emma Wilson for a year and then taught in several schools.

Through her teaching and community work, Mary McLeod learned a great deal about the care and education of children. While teaching in Sumter, South Carolina, she met and married Albertus Bethune. He was a teacher in the same school where Mary McLeod taught. They moved to Savannah, Georgia, to teach. Their son, Albert McLeod Bethune, was born there.

Mary McLeod Bethune was interested in opening a school in a place where a school would be greatly needed. In 1904 she rented a two-story, frame building and opened a school for girls in Daytona Beach, Florida. She started her school with one dollar and fifty cents in her pocket. The first students in the class were five girls and her own son. Using the tuition money paid by the students, Mrs. Bethune was able to pay the rent on the building for the first month.

Her school grew rapidly, and in less than two years she had 250 students. The school was called the Daytona Normal and Industrial School for Negro Girls. As the years passed, Mrs. Bethune acquired additional land. Some of the land was used for growing food, and more buildings were also added to the school. By 1923 the school merged with a men's college called Cookman Institute and became the Bethune-Cookman Collegiate Institute. Mary Bethune served as president of the school. Today, the school, now called Bethune-Cookman College, has a campus of many acres and graduates a great many students.

In addition to directing the special division of the National Youth Administration, Mrs. Bethune served as President Franklin Roosevelt's Special Adviser on Minority Affairs. During the presidency of Harry Truman, Mary Bethune was appointed by the State Department as an official consultant. One of her most important assignments was to attend the conference which drafted a charter for the United Nations.

In 1955 Mary McLeod Bethune died quietly in her home in Daytona Beach, Florida. She was buried on the campus of Bethune-Cookman College. Mrs. Bethune devoted her entire life to improving the educational opportunities for black people. She served her country well.

Reviewing the Story

Fill in each blank with the word or words which completes each sentence correctly.

1. Mary McLeod's older brothers and sisters were born _____,

   but she was born _____.

2. Mary McLeod and the other children in the family worked in the _____

   and _____ fields.

3. When Mary McLeod attended Emma Wilson's school, she had to walk _____

   _____ each way to school.

4. A _____ helped to pay for Mary McLeod's education at Scotia Seminary.

5. Mary McLeod wanted to do _____ work in Africa.

6. When Mary McLeod Bethune began her school, she had _____ students in her first class.

7. During the presidency of _____, Mrs. Bethune served as Special Adviser on Minority Affairs.

8. In 1923 the Daytona Normal and Industrial School for Negro Girls merged with _____.

Finding Synonyms

Match each word in Column A with its synonym in Column B. Write the correct letter of the synonym on the blank before each word in Column A.

	Column A		Column B
1.	_____special	a.	grounds
2.	_____additional	b.	quick
3.	_____rapid	c.	chosen
4.	_____merge	d.	counselor
5.	_____adviser	e.	supplementary
6.	_____campus	f.	unique
7.	_____selected	g.	begun
8.	_____started	h.	combine

General Colin L. Powell

NATIONAL SECURITY ADVISER AND CHAIRMAN OF THE JOINT CHIEFS OF STAFF

On October 1, 1989, President Bush swore in Colin L. Powell as Chairman of the Joint Chiefs of Staff. Powell would be the highest ranking officer in the United States military. He was the first black man to head the U.S. Armed Forces.

Colin Powell was born in Harlem in 1937. His parents were Jamaican immigrants. They worked hard so their children could have a better life. Colin knew his parents expected him to be successful.

After high school Colin went to City College in New York. There Colin signed up for the ROTC, the Reserve Officers Training Corp. Colin liked everything about the ROTC. He liked the discipline, the uniforms, and the studies. Soon Colin's instructors and classmates realized that he was a natural leader. Colin graduated with the ROTC's highest rank, cadet colonel.

After college Colin went into the army. He dreamed of commanding troops. Colin was sent to Georgia for training. Life in Georgia was different from life in New York. Colin could not even order a hamburger at the drive-in. Blacks were required to go to the back door. Colin would not go to the back door for anything.

Colin was ordered in 1962 to go to Vietnam as a military adviser. The U.S. was helping South Vietnam resist becoming part of communist North Vietnam. In Vietnam Colin and his battalion searched for enemy soldiers. One day they were walking through a rice paddy. Colin stepped on a Punji stick, a sharpened stake hidden in the water by the enemy. It went all the way through his foot! Colin was awarded a Purple Heart.

Powell was back in Vietnam in 1968 when a helicopter he was riding in crashed. Colin jumped free of the helicopter. He could see the engine smoking, and he knew it might explode at any minute. Powell thought of the men inside who were injured too badly to move. He went back into the helicopter again and again, pulling four men to safety. He was awarded the Soldier's Medal for his heroism.

In 1972 Lieutenant Colonel Powell was asked by one of his superiors to apply to be a White House Fellow. The best officers from all the armed forces competed for the fellowship. Fellows were given jobs at the highest levels of the government. Colin was accepted! He was given the job of assistant in the Office of Management and Budget. He impressed everyone with his cheerful personality, hard work, and intelligence.

After his fellowship ended, Colin's dream of commanding troops came true. He was put in charge of an infantry battalion in Korea. After his command in Korea, Powell was reassigned to Washington. Colin used the opportunity to educate himself. He enrolled in the National War College.

In 1986 Powell, now a general, had just taken command of the Fifth Corps in Germany when he got a call from one of his old bosses at the Pentagon, Frank Carlucci. Carlucci had just been named national security adviser to President Reagan. He would be in charge of advising the president on all military matters, and he needed a deputy he could count on. He asked Powell to take the job, but Colin refused. He didn't want to give up his command. When President Reagan called Powell himself, Colin agreed to take the job.

When Carlucci was promoted to secretary of defense, one man was a clear choice to take his place as national security adviser—Colin Powell. Powell became the first black man to hold this powerful position.

After Reagan's term ended, Powell got a call from the new president. President Bush wanted to appoint his own national security adviser. But Powell wasn't out of a job for long. On October 1, 1989, President Bush appointed Powell Chairman of the Joint Chiefs of Staff. Powell now held the highest military position in the United States.

Powell's time as chairman was not quiet. First he directed Operation Just Cause against the dictator of Panama, Manuel Noriega. Then came Operation Desert Storm against Saddam Hussein of Iraq. The American people became used to seeing Powell on TV. He calmly and clearly explained U.S. military strategy.

In October of 1993, Powell retired as Chairman of the Joint Chiefs of Staff. The young man from City College had made it to the very top of the United States Armed Forces. More importantly, he had won and kept the respect of soldiers, presidents, and the American people.

Reviewing the Story

Fill in each blank with the word or words which completes each sentence.

1. Colin Powell's parents immigrated to the United States from _____.

2. At City College Colin's instructors and classmates in ROTC soon realized he

   was a natural _____.

3. After Colin graduated from college, the army sent him to _____ to

   receive further _____.

4. In _____ Colin and the battalion he advised looked for

   _____ soldiers hidden in the jungle.

5. While he was walking through a rice paddy, Colin stepped on a Punji

   _____, a sharpened stake hidden underwater.

6. Powell was awarded the Soldier's Medal for pulling four injured men out a

   _____ that had crashed in Vietnam.

7. President _____ called Colin Powell to ask him to accept a

   position as deputy to the national security adviser.

8. On October 1, 1989, President Bush appointed Colin Powell as _____

   _____, the highest military position in

   the nation.

Finding Synonyms

Match each word in Column A with its synonym in Column B. Write the correct letter of the synonym on the blank before each word in Column A.

Column A   Column B

1. _____ adviser   a. helper

2. _____ instructor   b. hurt

3. _____ injured   c. peaceful

4. _____ accept   d. leap

5. _____ jump   e. teacher

6. _____ assistant   f. counselor

7. _____ quiet   g. lead

8. _____ command   h. take

Gwendolyn Brooks

POET

Gwendolyn Brooks, an American poet and Pulitzer Prize winner, was born on June 7, 1917, in Topeka, Kansas. When she was a month old, her family moved to Chicago. She grew up and went to school in Chicago and still lives there.

Gwendolyn was a bright little girl. She had a keen mind, and she wanted to learn anything and everything about the world around her. She asked many questions—almost too many, her mother often thought. But her parents knew how to guide such an active and inquiring child. They wanted her to go to school and learn all she possibly could. They encouraged her to read and to think.

Gwendolyn's teachers could see that she had a talent for writing. From her reading, she developed a very large vocabulary. She also loved to talk and never seemed to have any trouble expressing herself. Her teachers encouraged her to write poetry, and her first poem was published when she was thirteen.

Art and music were always a part of Gwendolyn Brooks's daily life. Gwendolyn's mother enjoyed playing and writing music. Her father worked in a music publishing house. Her brother, Raymond, was an artist. This kind of home life was good for Gwendolyn. Each member of the family helped her to become an artistic person.

Gwendolyn Brooks always needed to be busy to be happy. After she finished junior college, she held several jobs doing general office work. She also worked for a newspaper and a magazine. Those who worked with or around her were impressed by her great ability to get things done quickly.

Although Gwendolyn Brooks had a natural talent for writing poetry, she studied and worked to make her writing better. She knew that she had a lot to learn. In Chicago she entered a class in poetry where she learned the fine points of being a writer. Her poems soon started to appear in national magazines, and in 1945 her first book of poems was published. In the same year she was honored by a national magazine as one of "Ten Women of the Year."

In 1950 Gwendolyn Brooks received her greatest literary award, the Pulitzer Prize, for her book of poems, *Annie Allen.* Each year writers who have shown the greatest talent in poetry and other forms of writing are given this prize. Gwendolyn Brooks was the first black woman to win a Pulitzer Prize.

Many people have given their reasons for the success of Gwendolyn Brooks. They have tried to explain why so many people are charmed by her work. They all agree that her work can be understood by everyone. She writes about the things that people think, see, and feel. She has written about her own experiences in life. This collection of writings, *Report from Part One,* was published in 1972.

Gwendolyn Brooks has her own ideas about what a good writer should be. She says that a writer must be able to see and understand people as they go about their daily lives. The writer must be able to see beauty where no beauty exists and then describe that beauty for others to see and enjoy. Gwendolyn Brooks follows her own advice about good writing. She has mastered the art of putting into words the happenings of life, whether happy or sad, so that all people can share these experiences with her.

Understanding the Story

Answer the following questions and statements by using the information given in the story.

1. How old was Gwendolyn Brooks when her first poem was published? _____

_____

2. In what way was Gwendolyn Brooks honored by a national magazine in 1945? ___

_____

3. What was the greatest literary award received by Gwendolyn Brooks? _____

_____

4. When was Gwendolyn Brooks's first book of poems published? _____

_____

5. List the things which Gwendolyn Brooks believes a good writer must be able to do.

_____

_____

_____

_____

6. Why can Gwendolyn Brooks's work be understood by everyone? ------------

----

----

7. What different musical and artistic activities did the Brooks family enjoy? ------------

----

Finding the Meanings

Match each word in Column A with its meaning in Column B. Write the correct letter of the meaning on the blank before each word in Column A.

Column A

1. ------------literary

2. ------------inquire

3. ------------artistic

4. ------------national

5. ------------publish

6. ------------guide

7. ------------keen

8. ------------general

Column B

a. having or showing appreciation of beauty

b. common to many or most

c. to make publicly known

d. having to do with literature

e. bright and alert

f. to search for information

g. to lead or direct

h. belonging to a whole nation

Shirley Chisholm

UNITED STATES REPRESENTATIVE

"Fighting Shirley Chisholm," as she is called by her friends and associates, battled her way to winning a seat in Congress during 1968. By winning, she became the first black woman ever to be elected to a seat in the United States Congress.

Shirley Anita St. Hill was born in Brooklyn, New York, in 1924. She learned to talk and walk early and could read and write before she was five. By the time she was nearly three, she enjoyed giving orders to all the other children around her.

Shirley's mother was a seamstress, and her father worked as a baker's helper and later a factory hand. Her parents found it difficult financially to take care of a family of five. When Shirley St. Hill was three years old, her mother took her and her two sisters to Barbados to live on their grandmother's farm. The children lived with their grandmother until Shirley St. Hill was eleven years old. They received a good early education in British-styled schools in Barbados.

After returning to Brooklyn, Shirley St. Hill continued her schooling. She became vice-president of a girls' honor society, graduated from high school in 1942, and was offered several scholarships.

She went to Brooklyn College the following fall. Shirley St. Hill had decided that she would become a teacher. She majored in sociology. Her political science professor, Louis Warsoff, saw the ability and spirit she showed as a student. He told her that she ought to go into some area of politics. Shirley St. Hill graduated from college in 1946 with honors.

After graduation, she found it very difficult to find a teaching job because she looked younger than her age. The Mt. Calvary Child Care Center in Harlem realized her potential ability and hired her as a teacher's aide. Shirley St. Hill continued working and studying and became a teacher at the center. She worked for the center for seven years. During that time, she attended evening classes at Columbia University to work for a master's degree in early childhood education.

Shirley St. Hill met Conrad Chisholm at Columbia University while attending classes. They were married in 1949. In 1953 she became the director of a private nursery school. After a year she was offered the directorship of a child care center in Manhattan, and she spent the next several years supervising a staff of 24 teachers and other personnel. In 1959 Shirley Chisholm became educational consultant for New York City's Bureau of Child Welfare.

Shirley Chisholm was drawn to politics, and she ran for president of a political organization in 1958, but she lost. In 1960 a group of six persons, including Shirley Chisholm, formed the Unity Democratic Club. They backed chosen candidates for political elections in their assembly district. Their slate lost, but they began planning for the 1962 elections.

In 1964 Mrs. Chisholm ran for a vacant state assembly seat in Brooklyn. She faced opposition because she was a woman, but she won and went to Albany as a member of the New York State Assembly. The voters showed their confidence in Shirley Chisholm when she had to run for re-election in both 1965 and 1966 because of changes in the district lines. She won both general elections.

In 1968 Shirley Chisholm became a candidate in the United States Congressional race. She and the people backing her worked long, hard hours.

She wanted to prove that she could win the election without compromising her beliefs. She won the primary and general election, and lived up to her campaign slogan, "Fighting Shirley Chisholm— Unbought and Unbossed."

During her first year in the House, Shirley Chisholm showed her independent spirit by refusing to accept her assignments to House subcommittees dealing with forestry and family farms. She felt that they offered little opportunity for her to serve the poor people she was representing. She was finally reassigned to the Veterans' Affairs Committee and to subcommittees on education and training. Representative Chisholm believed that poverty, inadequate housing, and poor education were some of the most important problems facing the people.

In 1971 Shirley Chisholm entered the race for the Democratic Party's presidential nomination. She had no illusions about her chances of winning. She entered the race with the aim of forcing people to take seriously a representative of two groups—women and blacks.

Shirley Chisholm retired from the House of Representatives in 1982. In 1983 she accepted a new challenge. She was named Purington Professor at Mount Holyoke College. At Mount Holyoke Shirley Chisholm could pass on her knowledge of politics and her fighting spirit to a new generation.

Finding the Meanings

Choose the word and write it in the blank following its correct meaning.

difficult

vacant

return

supervise

independent

potential

confidence

associate

1. free or self-determining   _____

2. a partner or colleague   _____

3. hard to do or accomplish   _____

4. firm belief or trust   _____

5. to look after and direct   _____

6. capable of coming into being   _____

7. unfilled or unoccupied   _____

8. to go back   _____

Understanding the Story

Match the beginning part of each sentence in Column A with its ending in Column B. Write the correct letter of the ending on the blank before each beginning in Column A.

Column A

1. _____ In 1968 Shirley Chisholm won

2. _____ Shirley's mother worked

3. _____ Education in Barbados was

4. _____ By the time she was five years old,

5. _____ At Brooklyn College,

6. _____ Shirley St. Hill's father worked

7. _____ Shirley and her sisters lived

8. _____ During high school,

Column B

a. in British-styled schools.

b. Shirley St. Hill majored in sociology.

c. with their grandmother in Barbados.

d. a seat in the U. S. Congress.

e. Shirley St. Hill was vice-president of an honor society.

f. as a seamstress.

g. Shirley could read and write.

h. as a baker's helper.

Nat King Cole

SINGER-ENTERTAINER

Nat King Cole was a man of many talents. He was a jazz pianist, a singer, a radio and television star, a movie star, and the head of his own business firm. He was also a husband and a proud father.

Nat King Cole was given the name Nathaniel Adams Coles when he was born March 17, 1919. He later changed his family name from Coles to Cole. He was the son of a Montgomery, Alabama, Baptist minister. Later his family moved to Chicago, where he grew up with his sister and three brothers. Nat and the other children of the Coles family were very close to each other.

In the Coles family each person had a job to do around the house. The children worked together to make the beds, wash the dishes, and help their mother clean the house. But Mrs. Coles knew that her children needed to learn more than just how to clean house. In addition to helping them with their homework from school, Mrs. Coles gave music lessons to Nat and the other Coles children.

Mrs. Coles hoped that Nat would be-come a great pianist. But like most other children his age, Nat did not always want to practice his piano lessons. So Mrs. Coles often played the piano with Nat and helped him to enjoy his piano prac-tice. Nat King Cole never forgot his mother's help. On one of his television shows he praised his mother by saying, "My mother was the only real music teacher I ever had."

Nat was very young when he began to show real talent for music. By the time he was four, he had learned to play sev-eral simple songs. At the age of twelve, he was playing the piano and singing in his father's church.

Nat King Cole became a professional pianist even before he finished high school. His brother Eddie organized a band called the "Rogues of Rhythm." Nat played the piano with the band and earned about eighteen dollars a week. He often played until 2:00 a.m. Getting to school on time was often a problem.

This night job was against their fath-er's wishes. Mr. Coles compared the church and nightclubs to oil and water

—almost impossible to mix. He told Nat that he could not do both. He had to choose one or the other. Nat chose to become an entertainer. In time his father got used to the idea and accepted it.

Throughout his career, Nat King Cole remembered the teachings of his father. This famous entertainer was always an honest, down-to-earth person who loved to help others. His father had taught him to respect other people. In later years Nat King Cole even used the title of one of his father's sermons, "Straighten Up and Fly Right," as the name of a popuar song.

The road to success was rocky for Nat King Cole. He found that being an entertainer required hard work and extra effort. But he was willing to work hard. He also learned that a person usually has to start at the bottom with low pay and work his way to the top. Nat Cole wanted to succeed, and he knew that he could do it. One of his first steps to success came about in 1937 when he formed the King Cole Trio. The trio had its ups and downs but managed to stay together. During the next ten years, the King Cole Trio reached the top of the list of jazz groups.

Nat King Cole never intended to become a singer. He felt that he couldn't sing. He often said that he sounded like a frog. He might not have become a singer if it had not been for a nightclub patron who had had too much to drink. One night he demanded that Cole sing a song. Cole refused, but the owner of the club asked that he please the customer. Everyone, including Nat, was surprised. He didn't sound bad at all. In fact, everyone liked his voice. After that, Nat King Cole was no longer just a pianist—he was a singer, too.

Cole began to record his songs, and he sold millions of records. Such songs as "The Christmas Song," "Nature Boy," "Mona Lisa," and "Too Young" became best sellers throughout the country.

Nat Cole liked people, and they liked him. He worked with famous actors and other entertainers in the show world. He was respected by everyone—regardless of race—as a talented man who loved to make others happy.

Nat King Cole had three loves—his family, music, and baseball. He loved sports and was a great fan of the Los Angeles Dodgers. He had a permanent seat in Dodger Stadium. He helped sponsor a Los Angeles Little League team. He gave part of the profits from his record sales to Little League organizations in California. He once joked, "If I hadn't become a singer, I would have tried to become a baseball player."

In the last few years of his career, Nat Cole began to appear in musical shows. He gave up nightclub work. He wanted to entertain everyone—children as well as adults. And he knew that children could not go to nightclubs. Through these musical shows, he could reach more of the people he wanted to entertain.

Throughout his career, Nat King Cole worked to make people happy and to help people understand others. He recognized the differences between the many races and groups that live in America. But he felt that by entertaining people he could gain more respect for his race and help bring about the simple understanding and respect that each person should have for others.

Although show business demanded most of his time, Nat King Cole was a lonely man. While traveling with his shows, he missed his family. After he had worked hard and had become a successful entertainer, Nat Cole stopped traveling so much. He wanted to stay with and enjoy his family. He was the happiest when he was with his wife Maria, helping her with their five children.

Because of his career, Nat Cole touched many lives in many different ways. At the time of his death, February 15, 1965, he was one of the most famous black people in world history. The sound of his soft, smooth voice will be remembered for years to come. By those who knew him well, he is remembered as "a gentleman—a real nice guy."

Reviewing the Story

Fill in each blank with the word or group of words which completes each sentence correctly.

1. Nat's mother hoped that he would become a _____ .

2. Nat's brother organized a band called the "_____ ."

3. In 1937 Nat King Cole formed the _____ Trio.

4. Nat King Cole's three loves in life were _____ , _____ ,

   and _____ .

5. Nat loved sports and helped sponsor a _____

   _____ .

Finding Synonyms

Choose the correct synonym and write it in the blank following each word.

like	opposed	endless	ability	performer
easy	threesome	support	truthful	planned

1. sponsor _____

2. intended _____

3. simple _____

4. honest _____

5. enjoy _____

6. permanent _____

7. talent _____

8. against _____

9. entertainer _____

10. trio _____

Understanding the Story

Answer the following questions and statements from the information given in the story.

1. List three ways in which Nat's mother was especially helpful to him during his

   childhood. _____

   _____

   _____

   _____

2. What work did Nat Cole's father do? _____

   _____

3. Was the King Cole Trio successful? _____

   _____

4. List five of the many talents Nat King Cole possessed. _____

   _____

   _____

   _____

5. Why did Nat Cole give up nightclub work and begin appearing in musical shows?

   _____

   _____

Dean Dixon

SYMPHONY CONDUCTOR

The life of a symphony conductor is one of the hardest in the musical world. Many musicians dream of being great conductors, but very few are able to reach their goals. Dean Dixon has reached the top. At the age of twenty-six he was a guest conductor of the New York Philharmonic Symphony Orchestra. Never before had a black person been in this position. The old saying, "It can't happen here," was proved not always to be true.

Dean Dixon was born in 1915 in New York City. His family was not rich but had most of the things that a family needs. His father was born in Jamaica and finished law school in England. However, he worked as a bellhop in the United States. He died while Dean Dixon was a child.

When Dean was a small child, he and his mother often attended concerts at Carnegie Hall. She loved music and went to the symphony as often as she could afford to go. Dean Dixon still remembers stumbling up many long steps to reach the balcony so that they could hear a concert. His little legs were short, but he made it with the help of his mother's hand. At that age he did not always stay awake. In spite of the music he would become sleepy. But as he became older, Dean Dixon looked forward to going to concerts as much as his mother did.

Dean Dixon's musical training came early in his life. By the time he was able to read ordinary books, he could also read music. When he was six years old, he started taking violin lessons. After a few years his teacher felt that Dean was not suited to the violin. His mother did not agree and changed teachers. After this, little Dean began to make great progress in music.

Mrs. Dixon was a very wise mother. She wanted her child to develop good habits, to get along well with other people, and to do something worthwhile with his life. She saw to it that he engaged in wholesome activities. She was a great church worker, and she often met and worked with the neighborhood girls and boys. Mrs. Dixon's way of life inspired her son very much. Under her guidance,

Dean learned to enjoy art, music, and other cultural programs.

Music continued to charm Dean Dixon. His mother had given him a start, and he continued on his own. He played in his high school orchestra. Before graduating from high school, Dean had organized a little orchestra of his own. It met and practiced at the YMCA in Harlem. Dean was the conductor. He spent the little money that he had to buy music for the group. Since he didn't have enough money for a baton, he directed with a pencil. His orchestra was open to everyone—adult and child, black and white, male and female.

When Dean Dixon graduated from high school, he applied for admission to the Juilliard School of Music, one of America's best schools of music. He was examined by a famous conductor, Walter Damrosch, who quickly saw that Dixon showed great promise. Dixon continued to study violin, but he wanted to be a conductor more than anything else. He developed great skill in this field. After graduating from Juilliard, Dixon went to Columbia University for more study in conducting.

While Dean Dixon was in college, he continued to work with his interracial orchestra. This group became known as the Dean Dixon Symphony Society. A committee of women sponsored the orchestra. Free tickets were given to schoolchildren. Dixon was trying to bring classical music into the lives of children who lived on jazz alone. He was successful in doing this.

At the young age of twenty-three, Dean Dixon was invited to conduct a Town Hall concert for the League of Music Lovers. Later, in Harlem, his own orchestra played a whole program of works of Beethoven, Haydn, and Tchaikovsky. By this time his orchestra had seventy members. The youngest member was twelve and the oldest seventy-two. Many famous people came to the concert. Eleanor Roosevelt, the wife of the president of the United States, was in the audience. The head of the National Broadcasting Company was there, too. At the end of the concert, he invited Dixon to be guest conductor of the NBC Summer Symphony. After this he was invited to conduct many other musical groups.

Dean Dixon is an artist who has always loved a challenge. As a special project, Dixon became the leader of the National Youth Administration Orchestra. This was not an easy task. Keeping a large group of active youngsters still is a job in itself. To get them to produce good music is often impossible. But Dean Dixon had a way with them. He was firm but patient. He would laugh with them but could be serious, too. There was a time for hard work and a time for play. The young people loved and respected him.

In 1944 Dean Dixon organized the American Youth Orchestra. Its members were real artists. A critic, Olin Downes of the *New York Times,* praised their performances. He said that Dean Dixon had "the stuff of a real conductor."

Dean Dixon had many ideas for bringing music to the public. His orchestra gave "Concerts for Three-Year-Olds." Young children were allowed to sit on stage beside the musicians as they performed. He also started a series of "Symphonies at Midnight." These concerts were for working people who could not attend programs during regular hours.

For his work in helping young people, Dean Dixon received an "Award of Merit." He continued his work as long as he could. But as his program grew, costs increased also. The public was unable to support his projects, so Dean Dixon had to seek other means of earning a living.

It was at this time that Dixon received an invitation from an orchestra in Paris to serve as a musical director. As he became better known, he received offers from other countries. From 1952 to 1954 he was head conductor of the Swedish Goteborg Symphony. He was the first American to fill that post.

Dean Dixon conducts three months in Australia and five months in Germany. He is the musical director of the Sydney, Australia, Symphony Orchestra and has a contract with the Frankfurt Radio Symphony in Germany. He makes guest appearances in his spare time. Sometimes Dixon has engagements for five years in advance.

There is no doubt that Dean Dixon is a hard worker. He begins work at six in the morning. He works six to eight hours conducting and eight to ten hours planning and doing paper work. It has been said that he loses up to seven pounds in one concert.

Dean Dixon is an unselfish person. He has always felt that music should be used as a means of helping others. His orchestras have always been open to all qualified people. He has helped and encouraged many American composers and performers. Dixon has introduced new works by many unknown composers.

Called "America's Musical Ambassador," Dean Dixon carries goodwill and good music wherever he goes. He is a symbol for others of his race to enter the field of conducting. He has opened the door for others to follow.

Finding Antonyms

The words listed below appear in the story. Write an antonym for each of the words.

1. encourage _____

2. top _____

3. continue _____

4. often _____

5. remember _____

6. respect _____

7. wise _____

8. serious _____

Reviewing the Story

Fill in each blank with the word or group of words which completes each sentence correctly.

1. When Dean Dixon was _____ years old, he was a guest conductor of the New York Philharmonic Symphony Orchestra.

2. As a child, Dean and his mother attended concerts at _____
_____ .

3. At the age of six, Dean began taking _____ lessons.

4. While still in high school, Dean organized an _____ of his own.

5. In 1944 Dixon organized and conducted the _____

_____.

6. Dean loved the violin but wanted to be a _____ more than anything else.

7. Dean Dixon started a series of "_____" for working people.

8. Dean Dixon received an "_____" for his good work with young people.

Frederick Douglass

FIGHTER FOR FREEDOM

"Why am I a slave? Why are some people free while others are slaves?" These words were spoken by Frederick Douglass when he was a small child. As he grew older, these questions still burned in his mind. When he became an adult, he devoted his life to fighting for the rights of all people. As his chief weapon, he used his great gift of speech.

Frederick Douglass was born in the backwoods of Maryland about 1817. His real name was Frederick Augustus Washington Bailey, but he later changed his name to Douglass. Like many other slaves, Frederick did not know the exact date of his birth. Slaves usually knew only that they were born during some special season like plantingtime, harvesttime, winter, or summer.

Although Frederick Bailey was born a slave, his early childhood was fairly happy. Until the age of seven Frederick lived with his grandmother, Betsey Bailey. Grandmother Bailey took care of most of the black children on the plantation. Harriet Bailey, Frederick's mother, could not care for him. She too was a

slave and had to work on a plantation twelve miles away from Grandmother Bailey's house. Frederick saw his mother only a few times in his life. To see him, his mother had to walk the roundtrip distance of twenty-four miles. She could go to see her son only after she had finished her day's work. By the time she had a short visit with her son and then walked back to her plantation, it was sunrise and time for another day of work.

Frederick missed his mother, but Grandmother Bailey took good care of him. She did not have to work in the fields like the other slaves, so she and Frederick spent many happy hours together. She took him fishing, told him stories, and even taught him to sing. Grandmother Bailey also tried to explain slavery to him, for she wanted to prepare him for his life as a slave. She knew that when he became seven years old, he would be taken from her and sent to work as a slave.

Frederick's happy times with his grandmother soon came to an end. He was taken from her and sent to work on the plantation. Although he lived in a cabin with other slave children, he felt alone. He missed his grandmother.

Soon Frederick learned all about slavery. He learned that slaves had very few privileges. Even when his mother was dying, Frederick was not allowed to go to see her. He began to hate slavery more and more. "Will I ever be free?" he often asked himself.

Then Frederick found a new friend. When his master's daughter, Miss Lucretia, came to visit her father, Frederick was told to run errands for her. She liked his polite manner of doing his work, and she was kind to him. For the first time in his life, Frederick had a friend who was not a slave.

Miss Lucretia liked Frederick so much that she decided to take him to Baltimore. She wanted him to live in the home of her brother-in-law and take care of her little nephew. Frederick was very excited about the trip. But he was even more excited when she promised him some new clothes. Frederick had never owned anything new. He had always been given old clothes that were too small for older boys. He was so excited about the trip that he bathed in the river all day. He wanted to be nice and clean for his new clothes and his new home in Baltimore.

Frederick liked his new home. Mrs. Auld, the wife of his new master, treated him almost like a member of the family. She often invited Frederick to listen as she read the Bible to her son. Frederick loved to hear her read, and he asked her to teach him to read. So every day after the work was finished, Frederick was given a reading lesson.

When Mr. Auld heard about the reading lessons, he was very angry. He did not believe that slaves should be taught to read. Mrs. Auld stopped teaching Frederick, but he continued to study in secret. The white children in the neighborhood became his teachers. They helped Frederick learn many new words.

When Frederick was thirteen, he bought a book with money that he had earned by shining shoes. He read this book over and over again. There were stories about liberty and freedom in this book. The stories made him want to be free. He also found old newspapers that had stories about free people and how they lived. He would copy the words that he did not know. Later he would ask someone what the words meant. From his reading, Frederick learned that many white people hated slavery, too. Each story gave him hope. One day he would escape to freedom.

Although Frederick enjoyed reading, he did not like his master. Mr. Auld often had trouble getting Frederick to do what he was told to do. When Mr. Auld could not control Frederick, he sent him to the farm of a slave breaker. The slave breaker was a person who beat the slaves and made them work. He made the slaves afraid to do anything wrong.

What a terrible year that was for Frederick! He had trouble handling the farm animals and received many beatings because of his mistakes. But instead of breaking his spirit, each beating seemed to make him stronger. He was more determined to be free.

When the year with the slave breaker was up, Frederick was sent to work for a new master. Frederick worked hard, but he wanted to be free. He planned how he would escape.

During his second year with his new master, Frederick and five other slaves decided to run away. But their attempt to escape was not successful. After he was caught, Frederick was sent to work in a shipyard. There he became a skillful worker.

After working in the shipyard for a few months, Frederick again decided to run away. Dressed as a sailor and using borrowed seaman's papers, Frederick boarded a train for New York. He was twenty-one years old and on his way to freedom.

Frederick began looking for a job as soon as he reached New York, but jobs were not easy to find. However, he soon made some friends who were able to help him.

After a few months in New York, Frederick met Anna Murray, a black girl from Baltimore. Soon they were married and on their way to Massachusetts, where Frederick found work. He changed his name from Frederick Bailey to Frederick Douglass so that he could not be traced. Slave catchers were everywhere. Until he paid for his freedom, Frederick Douglass was in danger of being caught.

Frederick Douglass loved his freedom, and he wanted to help other slaves to be free. Douglass attended meetings where people spoke against slavery. At one meeting Douglass was asked to tell about his life as a slave. He was afraid. He had never spoken before a large group—and never to white people. But the people liked him so much that he was invited to travel and make more speeches.

Frederick Douglass continued to speak against slavery. But when he published a book about his life as a slave, he made the mistake of naming his owner, Mr. Auld. Soon Mr. Auld sent slave catchers to bring Frederick back to Baltimore.

To escape the slave catchers, Frederick Douglass went to England. People in England asked him to stay and to send for his family, but Douglass refused. America was his home, and he felt that he had to go back and help other slaves become free. His friends in England raised money so that Douglass could buy his freedom from Mr. Auld. The friends also gave Douglass money to help gain the freedom of other slaves.

When Douglass returned to America, he started printing his own newspaper. His wife and children helped with the printing. He called his paper *The North Star*. This was a suitable name. Runaway slaves often looked in the sky for the North Star to guide them to the free states. His newspaper could also guide them to freedom.

Douglass believed in doing as well as talking. Instead of only urging slaves to escape, he gave them direct help. He was active in the Underground Railroad. This group helped slaves escape from the South to the free states and Canada.

At the beginning of the Civil War, Frederick Douglass advised President Lincoln to free the slaves. Douglass believed that if slaves were freed, they would rise to the Union cause. He helped recruit northern blacks as soldiers for the Union army.

After the war he became concerned about the newly freed people. He believed that education was the answer to the blacks' economic problems. His writings on education influenced Booker T. Washington, the founder of Tuskegee Institute.

Frederick Douglass held many responsible public offices. He was United States Marshal for Washington, D. C. Later he was appointed Recorder of Deeds for the District of Columbia. He became a Minister to Haiti. His work in these areas showed that he was not simply a rebel. He was willing to try to make the government which he supported work well.

When Frederick Douglass died on February 20, 1895, America lost a great leader. In addition to being a leader of the black people, he was also a champion of justice for all. Since Frederick Douglass believed so strongly in freedom and justice, he devoted his entire life to the struggle of gaining equal rights for all people. He believed that all people—

regardless of color, sex, or religion— should be treated with respect. He felt that every honest citizen of the United States should enjoy the opportunities for success and freedom in their daily lives.

Frederick Douglass was a "North Star." He did all that he could to point out the way to freedom to everyone.

Finding the Meanings

Choose the word and write it in the blank before its correct meaning.

privilege   special   terrible   errand

attempt   polite   mistake   secret

1. _____ out of the ordinary

2. _____ hidden from view or knowledge

3. _____ a trip made to carry a message or perform a task

4. _____ extremely unpleasant or dreadful

5. _____ a special benefit or favor

6. _____ courteous or attentive

7. _____ to understand wrongly

8. _____ to make an effort at

Reviewing the Story

Fill in each blank with the word or words which completes each sentence correctly.

1. As a small child Frederick lived with his grandmother, _____

   _____ .

2. When Frederick was _____ years old, he began working on a plantation.

3. Frederick met his _____ only a few times during his lifetime.

4. While living in _____ with his second master,

   _____ taught Frederick how to read.

5. The _____ time that Frederick tried to escape from slavery, he was caught and sent to work in a _____.

6. Frederick changed his last name from _____ to _____ so that he could not be traced by the slave catchers.

7. Frederick's friends living in _____ raised money so he could buy his freedom.

8. Frederick Douglass was born in _____ about 1817.

9. In New York, Frederick met and married _____.

10. *The North Star* was a _____ printed by Douglass to help the slaves.

Charles Richard Drew

SCIENTIST

Countless lives are saved today because of our many blood banks. Dr. Charles Drew was the director of the first American Red Cross Blood Bank. He was also one of the first authorities on blood plasma.

Charles Drew was a man of many talents. He was first an athlete, then a doctor of medical research, and finally a, teacher of doctors. Dr. Drew was a champion in each of these fields.

Charles Drew was born in Washington, D. C., on June 3, 1904. He was the oldest of five children. His parents tried to provide the best for their children. They also encouraged their children to do their best at all times. This Charles Drew tried to do throughout his life.

As a child, Charles did many of the things that active children like to do. He liked all kinds of sports and was a better athlete than most of the children he played with. He was a very good swimmer. Each Fourth of July Charles entered a swimming contest at one of the neighborhood pools. By the time he was eight, he had won four medals.

Charles developed many of his fine personal qualities while he was still in high school. He attended Dunbar High School in Washington. There students were given good foundations in citizenship, in addition to excellent training in English, mathematics, science, and other regular subjects. Charles was a good student. He did his lessons well so that he could take part in several sports. He starred in football, basketball, baseball, and track. He got letters in all of these sports and became the school's "all-'round athlete."

Charles Drew's four years at Amherst College followed the same pattern as his high school days. He engaged in every sport the school had to offer. When he graduated in 1926, he received a trophy as the most outstanding athlete during his four years in college.

After leaving Amherst, Charles Drew became director of athletics at Morgan College, a small college in Baltimore, Maryland. He coached several fine athletic teams, but he felt a need for doing something different with his life. When he developed an interest in medicine, he left Morgan College to attend medical school.

Since Charles Drew had always been so interested in athletics, he turned to medicine a little later in life than most doctors do. He entered medical school at McGill University in Montreal, Canada. Once there, he really found himself. Being a doctor, the very best, became his goal. A young teacher at McGill, John Beatie, became his close friend. The two men worked on research projects together and developed respect for one another. Drew graduated in 1933 with high honors.

After two years of special training, Dr. Drew became a teacher in the medical school at Howard University. He also served as an assistant in surgery. He developed a love for surgery and went on to Columbia University in New York City for more study in this field.

It is for his work done while at Columbia that the world remembers him best. Dr. Drew was interested in the study of blood and made a special study on "Banked Blood." Until that time very little had been done in this field of medicine. Dr. Drew developed a process whereby blood plasma could be processed and preserved. It could be shipped to distant places and used for transfusions in saving lives.

While Dr. Drew was completing his study of blood, England went to war. His friend John Beatie was working with blood transfusions in London. It was at his request that Dr. Drew was asked to direct the "Blood for Britain Project." This program provided plasma which was used to treat shock in wounded soldiers. Plasma often served as a workable substitute for whole blood.

Thousands of lives were saved during World War II because of Dr. Drew's system of preserving blood plasma. Donor stations were set up and developed by Dr. Drew. The American Red Cross used his system as a model for setting up the first American Red Cross Blood Bank. Dr. Drew was made director of their "Blood Program."

After the war was over, Dr. Drew returned to teaching at Howard University. He gave his position all the time and energy he had to give. He was a dedicated man and guided his students with a firm hand. He demanded the very best from his students who were training as surgeons.

When the United States sent a team of doctors on a tour of European countries to help improve medical care and instruction in hospitals, Dr. Drew was included in the group. This same spirit of concern was expressed by Dr. Drew in many civic activities. He belonged to many public service societies and even served on the board of his local YMCA.

When Dr. Drew died in 1950 at the age of forty-five, the entire medical world was stunned. He did not live very long, but the world is much richer because of him and his good work. Dr. Drew is an excellent example of a great American who did not work for financial gain for himself, but for the betterment of humanity.

Reviewing the Story

Fill in each blank with the correct word or words. Each answer will be used only once.

John Beatie	Washington, D.C.	Morgan College
transfusions	Columbia University	blood plasma
baseball	McGill University	four
swimmer	Howard University	teacher

1. Dr. Drew worked out a way for _____ to be processed and preserved.

2. After college, Charles Drew became director of athletics at _____ _____.

3. Blood plasma can be shipped long distances and used for _____.

4. Charles Drew attended medical school at _____ and graduated with honors.

5. While in high school, Charles received letters in football, basketball, track, and _____.

6. Charles Drew was born in _____.

7. Dr. Drew's most well-known and important work was done while he was studying at _____.

8. Charles Drew and _____ worked together on many medical research projects.

9. Dr. Drew taught in the medical school at _____.

10. Charles Drew was a very good _____ and won _____ medals by the time he was eight years old.

11. During his short lifetime, Dr. Drew was an athlete, a doctor of medical research, and a _____ of doctors.

Finding Homonyms

Homonyms are words that are pronounced alike but have different meanings and are spelled differently. Match each word in Column A with its homonym in Column B. Write the correct letter of the homonym on the blank before each word in Column A.

Column A

1. _____ our

2. _____ red

3. _____ their

4. _____ do

5. _____ by

6. _____ won

7. _____ for

8. _____ need

9. _____ so

10. _____ sent

Column B

a. one

b. knead

c. hour

d. cent

e. due

f. read

g. sew

h. there

i. fore

j. buy

Jean Baptiste Du Sable

CHICAGO'S FIRST SETTLER

Chicago, the windy city with over three million people, grew from a settlement built by Jean Baptiste Pointe Du Sable. Jean Du Sable, a black explorer and trader, has been called America's greatest "black pioneer."

The land that now holds Chicago was once an open prairie. It was a piece of land that no one seemed to want. The Indians passed over the land as they moved from one place to another. The Indians felt that the land was an impossible place. At times the weather there was damp and hot. At other times the icy air from the nearby lake was unbearable. Wild garlic grew along the banks of the river which flowed through this land. The smell of garlic was terrible. The Indians of that area called the land *Eschikagou.* This Indian word had two similar meanings—"river of wild onions" and "the place of the skunk."

When Jean Du Sable came into this deserted prairie, he was looking for a place to settle. He was a handsome black man, over six feet tall, with a very pleasant manner. He had a keen mind and a sharp eye. He could see some good in the unwanted, wasted land. He thought the prairie was in a good location, for he saw the land as a crossroad of travel and trade. Du Sable built his trading post and started the settlement that was later named Chicago.

No one is sure about Du Sable's date of birth. Most records say that he was born about 1745 in St. Marc, Haiti. His mother, Suzanne, was a beautiful slave girl. She lived on one of the plantations on the Virgin Islands. His father was a pirate who sailed on a ship called the *Black Sea Gull.* Du Sable's father stole Suzanne from her master and took her to Haiti. He married her, and Jean Du Sable was their only child.

Du Sable was a very daring young boy. After his mother died, Jean Du Sable was placed in a boarding school near Paris, France. He was not happy there and soon ran away. When he returned home, he found that his father was no longer a pirate. He had opened a warehouse and had become a merchant.

One day Jean Du Sable and a young

friend, Jacques, borrowed a boat and sailed for America. They wanted to buy goods for the warehouse. The two boys sailed into a hurricane, and their boat was wrecked. The boys were saved when another ship came by and rescued them. They were put ashore at New Orleans.

Because of the color of his skin, Du Sable was in danger of being captured and sold as a slave. But he made several friends in New Orleans. These friends hid him and helped him build a small boat. He and Jacques escaped up the Mississippi River. A Choctaw Indian guide who spoke many languages went with them as far as St. Louis.

St. Louis was a new fort and a great fur-trading center. Du Sable stayed in and about St. Louis for several years. He learned to speak the language of the Illinois Indian tribe. He also learned to live and hunt like an Indian. But Du Sable was restless. He soon left St. Louis and traveled up the Illinois River and across the Great Lakes into Canada.

When Du Sable returned to the Illinois territory, he lived in a small Indian village with the Potawatami tribe. Du Sable fell in love with an Indian girl, but he had to become a member of the tribe before he could marry her. Du Sable went through the tribal ceremonies that were required. Then he bought land and settled among the Indians as a farmer and a trader.

In 1772 Du Sable left the Indian village and built his fort on the present site of Chicago. He started trading with the Indians who had articles to barter. Soon he began to trade with merchants from other forts along Lake Michigan.

After building his fort, Du Sable built a five-room house for his family. He built one of the finest houses in that section of the country. His wife and son were proud of their house. All the Indians of his wife's tribe settled in the area.

Du Sable took great pride in building his settlement. Soon more buildings were added—barns, a forge, a mill, smokehouses, and several workshops. Other homes were built, and fields were planted. Du Sable's fort became the best one between St. Louis and Montreal, Canada.

Trouble has a way of happening in everyone's life, and Du Sable's life was no exception. He was arrested in 1778 during the conflict between the French, the Indians, and the British. At that time the French and British were enemies. Because of his French background, Du Sable was arrested and accused of being against the British. However, the British authorities could find no proof of this, and they had to set him free.

For a while Du Sable did not return to his fort. Instead, he became a guide. He knew the country, and he loved to travel. He became a guide for missionaries, trappers, hunters, and explorers. One Indian tribe respected him so much that they wanted to make him their chief. He was a friend of the great chief Pontiac and of Daniel Boone.

Du Sable returned to his home in 1784. He worked hard as a merchant and became a wealthy man. After several years Du Sable sold his land and moved with his family to St. Charles, Missouri. Through this small frontier town, many pioneers passed every day in their covered wagons. The pioneers were heading west in search of a better life. Du Sable wanted to explore new territories again, but he was too old to go. He was happy talking to pioneers who passed his way. Since many of the pioneers could not understand the Indian language, they depended on Du Sable to help them bargain and trade with the Indians.

Du Sable died about 1818. He was buried near the graves of other great pioneers. The memory of Chicago's "black pioneer" is kept alive by the records of the Chicago Historical Society.

Finding the Meanings

With the help of a dictionary, write a short meaning for each of the following words.

1. explorer ....

2. prairie ....

3. merchant ....

4. frontier ....

5. pirate ....

Understanding the Story

Write <u>true</u> or <u>false</u> before each of the following statements.

1. .... Du Sable was an enemy of Daniel Boone.

2. .... Later in life Du Sable moved with his family to St. Charles, Missouri.

3. .... Du Sable was born about 1690.

4. .... Du Sable was restless and enjoyed exploring new land.

5. .... Before marrying an Indian girl, Du Sable became a member of the Potawatami tribe.

6. .... Du Sable lived in New Orleans for many years.

Reviewing the Story

Fill in each blank with the word or words which completes each sentence correctly.

1. Jean Du Sable built a .... on open prairie land.

2. When Du Sable was a boy, his father was a ...., but later in life his father became a ....

3. When Jean Du Sable and a friend sailed for America their boat was .... during a ....

4. The settlement Du Sable started was later named _____.

5. During the years that he lived in the city of _____, Du Sable learned the language of the Illinois Indian tribe.

6. As more buildings were added to Du Sable's settlement, his fort became the best one between _____ and _____.

7. Most records say that Jean Du Sable was born about _____ in _____ _____.

8. After Jean Du Sable's mother died, he was placed in a boarding school near _____.

9. The memory of Jean Du Sable is kept alive by the records of the _____ _____.

10. Du Sable was buried near the graves of other great _____.

Toni Morrison

WRITER

Toni Morrison is a great writer. She creates literature that has meaning for all people. But that is only a part of what Toni Morrison does. She writes for black people about the lessons of history and the treasures of black culture.

Toni Morrison was born in 1931 in Lorain, Ohio. Her birth name was Chloe Anthony Wofford. The Great Depression had just started, and times were hard. Toni's father worked three jobs to feed his family. He barely made enough money to support them.

While Toni's family did not have much money, they were rich in other ways. Toni grew up hearing wonderful stories from her parents and grandparents. She heard folktales, stories about her family's life in the South, and stories about Africa. These stories made her feel proud to be black.

As Toni grew, her love of stories continued. Her parents taught her to read before she started school. She read many books by white writers. Toni thought it was wonderful that she could understand these books. After all, she

was from a different culture. Toni thought blacks should also write about black culture.

Toni's love of reading helped her become a good student. Still, her family did not expect her to continue her education after high school. Only one member of her family had ever attended college. But Toni had ideas of her own. She enrolled in Howard University, then an all-black school. Toni thought the other students would be excited about books and ideas. She was disappointed. Many of the students only cared about clothes and parties. A lot of people at Howard could not even pronounce her name, Chloe. She changed her name to Toni.

At Howard Toni joined a theater group, the Howard University Players. During the summers the group traveled throughout the South performing plays. At last Toni was able to see the land where her grandparents had lived as farmers. Toni could see that life was harder for blacks in the South than in the North. But Toni could also see that the black communities there were much like the ones she knew at home. Toni realized that all the black people in America were really just one big community.

After Toni graduated from Howard, she went to Cornell University. She earned her master's degree and became a professor at Texas Southern University. She taught there for two years and then joined the faculty of Howard University.

At Howard Toni met Harold Morrison. He was from Jamaica. They married and had two sons, but Toni was unhappy. The marriage was not a good one, and she often felt lonely. Toni began to write stories. At first she did not tell anyone what she was doing. She was careful to write when no one was around. Then she joined a writer's group. One day she brought a new story to the group. It was about a young black girl who wanted blue eyes.

By 1964 Toni's marriage was over. She took a job as an editor at Random House in Syracuse, New York. Toni was very lonely during this time. Again she turned to stories for strength. At night she began turning the story of the girl who wanted blue eyes into a novel. When she had it partly finished, Toni sent it to an editor. The editor told Toni she should finish the book. The novel, *The Bluest Eye*, was published in 1970.

In 1968 Toni was given a better editing job at Random House in New York City. There she worked to help young black writers publish their books. Some of these writers have become well-known. Toni also published books about black people. One of these was *The Black Book*. This book was Toni's idea. It is a scrapbook of pictures, journals, and other documents that tell about the lives of ordinary black people. Toni worked hard during the day, but she still found time to write at night.

Toni's second novel, *Sula*, was published in 1973. The book is about two friends— one of them quiet and shy, the other bold and rebellious. Again critics liked the book.

In 1976 Morrison began teaching at Yale University. She taught courses in writing and courses about the literature written by black authors. During this time she wrote her third novel, *Song of Solomon*. It won the National Book Critics' Circle Award, which is given to the best fiction book of the year. Her fourth novel, *Tar Baby*, followed in 1981. This novel, as well as *Song of Solomon*, sold many copies.

In 1984 Toni left her editing job. She became a visiting professor at the State University of New York in Albany. Later she moved to Princeton to teach writing and black studies.

Toni's fifth novel, *Beloved*, was published in 1987. It is based on a true story of a woman who had escaped from slavery. Beloved won a Pulitzer Prize. In 1992 Toni published her sixth novel, *Jazz*.

In 1993 Toni Morrison received one of the world's highest honors. She became the first black American to be awarded the Nobel Prize in Literature. At last Toni was recognized as one of the greatest writers now living.

Toni Morrison does not write for herself. She writes for her community. Toni believes black Americans need their own way of seeing themselves. The stories Toni heard as a girl made her proud to be black. Now Toni Morrison's beautiful words speak to everyone about the dignity of black Americans.

Reviewing the Story

Underline the word or group of words which completes each sentence correctly.

1. After high school Toni Morrison attended **(a) The University of Texas** **(b) Howard University**   **(c) Harvard University** .

2. In college Toni Morrison joined a group that traveled around **(a) playing music**   **(b) showing movies**   **(c) putting on plays** .

3. Toni's husband, Harold Morrison, came to the U.S. from **(a) Zimbabwe** **(b) Puerto Rico**   **(c) Jamaica** .

4. The name of Toni Morrison's first novel is **(a) *The Bluest Eye***   **(b) *The Black Book***   **(c) *The Song of the Stranger*** .

5. In 1984 Toni gave up her publishing job and became **(a) a blues singer** **(b) a professor**   **(c) an executive** .

6. Toni Morrison was recognized as a great writer when she was awarded the **(a) Grand Prize**   **(b) Iron Cross**   **(c) Nobel Prize** .

Finding Antonyms

Choose the correct antonym and write it in the blank following each word.

weakness   death   ended   poor

ashamed   easier   bold   never

1. birth ---------------------
2. rich ---------------------
3. proud ---------------------
4. harder ---------------------

5. strength ---------------------
6. often ---------------------
7. shy ---------------------
8. continued ---------------------

W. C. Handy

FATHER OF THE BLUES

W. C. Handy is perhaps best known as the person who wrote "St. Louis Blues." For many years this blues song was a popular favorite of millions of Americans. This song started W. C. Handy on the road to fame and made him thousands of dollars. Most of that money he spent while helping other musicians.

Handy was what many people would call a born musician. All forms of music interested him. His grandmother told him that his big ears meant that he had a talent for music.

W. C. Handy was born in Florence, Alabama, in 1873. His full name was William Christopher Handy. His father and grandfather were ministers, and they wanted him to be a minister, too. But young Handy had other ideas.

Handy once said that music was always a part of his life. As a child he said that he could hear music in the beauty of nature. He listened to the call of the birds and the sounds of the cattle in the pasture. Even the sounds of the frogs and owls seemed to be music for him. W. C. Handy tried to imitate these different

sounds in many of the songs he wrote.

In school William's favorite subject was music. His music teacher taught him many kinds of music. The school had no piano, but the teacher would sing to his students. The students sang and heard everything from gospel hymns to great works of opera.

William's father did not like music or musicians. He said that all musicians were sinful. He said musical instruments were the work of the devil. He did not allow a piano or organ in his church.

Little William did not accept his father's beliefs about music. He wanted to be a musician, so he began by making his own musical instruments. He played tunes on a fine-tooth comb. He beat rhythms on his mother's pots and pans. Later, after working as a water boy for a rock quarry, William was able to buy his first real instrument—a guitar. He was only twelve years old at the time. His parents were angry, and they told him to take it back to the store. They made him exchange it for a dictionary.

Handy received his first music lesson

on an instrument from a member of a traveling band. The man sold him an old cornet for $1.75 and showed him how to play it. Young William took the music lessons secretly.

One day, instead of going to school, Handy went out of town with the circus band. Without his father's knowing it, Handy had become a member of the group. He earned eight dollars. Handy thought that this would please his father. Instead of praise, he got a whipping.

When Handy was eighteen, he left his hometown and went to Birmingham. After studying for a while, he was able to pass the teacher examination. He then taught school for two years. Later, he gave up his position to take a job at a foundry in Bessemer, Alabama. He made more money there than he did teaching.

While in Bessemer, Handy organized a small musical group. He played with the group, but he never forgot the religious teachings of his father. On Sundays he always went to church and sang and played the trumpet with the church choir.

After a few months in Bessemer, Handy lost his job at the foundry. To support himself, he began to travel with his musical group. The group decided to go to Chicago. There was to be a World's Fair that year, and the men thought they might find work. They had no money, so they decided to hitch a ride on a freight train. The brakeman found them and put them off. They stood beside the tracks and began to sing sad songs. After hearing them sing, the brakeman felt sorry for them and let them ride in a boxcar.

The World's Fair was delayed for a year, so the quartet moved on to St. Louis. With no job and no money, the group soon separated. Handy had to sleep wherever he could. Many times he slept on the hay of the horse stalls at the race track. Nights were more lonely than days for Handy. The opening line from

his famous "St. Louis Blues" tells how he felt about those lonely nights: "I hate to see the evening sun go down."

Handy searched for better things to do. At times he felt like going home, but he did not want to face his father in defeat, so he traveled. To feed himself he did everything from paving streets to playing in local bands. While in Kentucky, Handy joined a successful minstrel group. This group traveled all over the United States. They even went to Mexico and Cuba.

Handy did not become successful until he stopped playing ordinary marches and waltzes. After listening to a group of young boys one night, Handy realized that people enjoyed hearing everyday music—music that was born in the cotton fields and on the river banks. This was the music he loved and knew best. This was the music of his people.

W. C. Handy wrote many blues songs. He also wrote and published many versions of Negro spirituals. He even wrote several articles and books about his kind of music. He loved music, and he shared that love with the entire world.

When Handy was almost eighty years old, he lost his eyesight. But he continued to perform in nightclubs and on radio and television. He helped many young actors and musicians by organizing the Negro Actors Guild and the W. C. Handy Foundation for the blind.

When Handy died in 1958 at an age of eighty-four, the mayor of St. Louis named April 10, 1958, W. C. Handy Day. Many tributes were given that day to the man who had added to the fame of St. Louis by writing a song about the city that meant so much to him.

W. C. Handy dedicated his life to writing the kind of music that permitted him and others like him to tell of their joys, their fears, their sad times, as well as their happy times. He believed that music was the key to universal understanding.

Reviewing the Story

Underline the word or group of words which completes each sentence correctly.

1. W. C. Handy was started on the road to fame when he wrote   **(a) "America"** **(b) "St. Louis Blues"**   **(c) "Hail to the Chief"** .

2. William's father and grandfather were   **(a) musicians**   **(b) writers**   **(c) ministers** .

3. The first instrument William bought was a   **(a) guitar**   **(b) drum**   **(c) piano** .

4. William was born in   **(a) Florida**   **(b) Mississippi**   **(c) Alabama** .

5. William's parents told him to take back the instrument he bought and exchange it for a   **(a) pair of shoes**   **(b) dictionary**   **(c) shirt** .

6. Handy received his first music lesson from   **(a) a teacher at school**   **(b) his brother**   **(c) a member of a traveling band** .

7. Many tributes were given to W. C. Handy when he died in   **(a) 1962**   **(b) 1958** **(c) 1952** .

8. "St. Louis Blues" is a   **(a) sad**   **(b) happy**   song.

Finding Homonyms

Match each word in Column A with its homonym in Column B. Write the correct letter of the homonym on the blank before each word in Column A.

Column A	Column B
1. ....road	a. bee
2. ....to	b. rote
3. ....born	c. borne
4. ....be	d. beet
5. ....hear	e. rode
6. ....wrote	f. here
7. ....heard	g. two
8. ....beat	h. herd

Patricia Roberts Harris

ATTORNEY AND BUSINESS LEADER

Patricia Roberts Harris's leadership in the civil rights movement and activities within the Democratic Party brought her name to President Lyndon B. Johnson's attention. As a result, in 1965 the president selected Patricia Harris to serve as Ambassador to Luxembourg. She became the first black woman to serve as a United States ambassador.

Patricia Roberts was born in 1924 in Mattoon, Illinois. Her early years were spent in Mattoon and Chicago, where she graduated from high school. She received five offers of college scholarships and decided on Howard University in Washington, D.C. During the next few years, she held a research assistantship and obtained her degree in 1945, graduating with an outstanding academic record.

After graduation, Patricia Roberts decided to continue her education. She spent the next two years doing graduate work in industrial relations at the University of Chicago. She was also employed as program director of the Young Women's Christian Association. During the

next few years, she returned to Washington for more graduate study, took a position as assistant director of the American Council on Human Rights, and served as executive director of a black sorority that has its national headquarters in Washington.

During all these busy years, Patricia Roberts married William Beasley Harris, who was then a member of the law faculty of Howard University. After her marriage, she entered George Washington University Law School.

After earning her law degree in 1960, Patricia Harris's first position with the United States government was as a trial attorney with the Department of Justice. She left the department after a year to accept an appointment as associate dean of students and lecturer in law at Howard University. She enjoyed this position since she believes that the study of law is excellent training for many other activities in life.

In July of 1963 President John F. Kennedy appointed her cochairperson of the National Women's Committee for

Civil Rights. One of her most important tasks was to help develop ways of broadening communication among the races. She also worked to create support among various women's groups for the civil-rights bill that was then before Congress. The knowledge she gained from her work with the N.A.A.C.P. helped her with these assignments. The following March, President Lyndon Johnson named her to the newly created Commission on the Status of Puerto Rico. Because of her great ability in dealing with others, she was well suited to the position.

It is no wonder, therefore, after her varied background, that the Senate quickly confirmed her appointment as Ambassador to Luxembourg. Patricia Harris seemed to communicate with the people of Luxembourg from the very beginning. They felt that she was warm and charming. Since the position took a great deal of her time, she had to give up positions in many other organizations. While serving as ambassador, President Johnson also named her an alternate delegate to the United Nations General Assembly in 1966 and 1967.

After returning to the United States, Patricia Harris has served in a variety of capacities. She became dean of the Howard University School of Law but left in 1970 to join a law firm in Washington, D.C., as a partner. And Patricia Harris's ability to work well with others has opened up new opportunities in the business world. In 1971 she became the first black woman to be named as a director of a major United States company. International Business Machines Corporation appointed her a director. Since then she has been appointed to other such posts.

Patricia Harris's sincerity, intelligence, and ability to work well with others brought her other opportunities. In 1972 she served as temporary chairperson of the credentials committee for the Democratic National Convention. Then in 1977 she became the first black woman to be appointed to the Cabinet. She served as secretary of the Department of Housing and Urban Development until 1979. Then she was appointed secretary of the Department of Health and Human Services, serving until 1981. Afterwards she remained active in both the political and business worlds. Patricia Harris died on March 23, 1985.

Reviewing the Story

Fill in each blank with the word or group of words which completes each sentence correctly.

1. In 1965 President Lyndon B. Johnson chose Patricia Roberts Harris to serve as

   _____ to _____.

2. Patricia Roberts received a scholarship for her college education and obtained a

   degree from _____ University.

3. After law school, Patricia Harris worked as a _____

   with the Department of _____.

4. The _____ confirmed Patricia Harris's appointment as ambassador.

5. Patricia Harris earned her law degree from _____

_____.

6. _____ Corporation

named Patricia Harris as a director of their company.

7. In 1970 Patricia Roberts Harris joined a _____ in Washington, D. C.

8. Patricia Harris's husband is _____,

and he is also an attorney.

Finding Synonyms

The words listed below appear in the story. Write a synonym for each of the words.

1. result _____

2. employed _____

3. early _____

4. various _____

5. ability _____

6. excellent _____

7. outstanding _____

8. temporary _____

William Henry Hastie

FEDERAL JUDGE

A judge has to decide cases based on the law. He must be fair to all people. William Henry Hastie is such a man. He was the first black person in the history of the United States to become a federal judge.

William Hastie was born in Knoxville, Tennessee, on November 17, 1904. He attended elementary school there before moving with his family to Washington, D. C. After completing high school in Washington, Hastie entered Amherst College in Massachusetts. He was a good student, and he graduated from Amherst in 1925 with high honors.

William Henry Hastie started his professional career as a teacher. He taught for two years at the Manual Training High School in Bordentown, New Jersey. Although he liked teaching, he wanted to be a lawyer. So he left his teaching position and entered Harvard Law School. He was again a good student, graduating with high honors in 1930.

Even as a very young man, William Henry Hastie was a fighter for equal rights for all people. But above all, he be-lieved in obeying the laws of his country.

After becoming a lawyer, Hastie used his legal talents to help other blacks. He became a teacher at Howard University Law School in Washington, D. C. He also joined a law firm. During the two years he was with the law firm, William Hastie learned a great deal about practical law. He also defended the rights of many black Americans.

Many important people heard about Hastie and the fine work he was doing. They liked the way he respected the law and the way he presented his cases in court. Because of Hastie's hard work and his ability to do a job well, Secretary of the Interior Harold Ickes appointed William Hastie as a government lawyer. Hastie did his job well in that department for four years. He devoted most of his time to helping people who could not help themselves.

One of the most important cases that he worked on was about the use of the oil-rich lands owned by the Osage Indians. Hastie worked to protect the rights of the Indians and their ownership of the land. He made sure that the Indians were treated justly and paid fairly for their oil and their land.

In another important case, Hastie worked to prevent hunters from killing too many reindeer in Alaska. The Eskimos of Alaska depend upon the reindeer's meat for food and its skin for clothing. Hastie knew that if too many reindeer were killed, they would soon vanish from the earth. Without the reindeer, the Eskimos would not have enough food to eat.

William Hastie later helped organize the Virgin Islands Company that provided jobs for the workers on the islands. He wrote the act that gave the people of the Virgin Islands their self-government.

President Franklin D. Roosevelt was impressed with Hastie's work. The president recognized that Hastie was a hard-working, honest man who believed in freedom and justice for all. In 1937 President Roosevelt appointed him judge of the District Court of the Virgin Islands.

Hastie was an immediate success as a judge. People liked him because they knew that he was a fair man. They knew that he believed in fair treatment and protection under the law. Hastie remained in the Virgin Islands as U. S. District Judge until 1939.

In 1939 William Hastie left the courtroom to become a law professor and the head of the Howard University Law School. He wanted to teach other blacks who were interested in becoming lawyers. Although he loved to teach young law students, in 1940 Hastie accepted an offer to serve as an adviser to the Secretary of War. Hastie's new job was to help improve the training conditions of black people in the armed services.

William Hastie was a man who believed in what he was doing. He believed that every person who was to fight in the United States Army should receive the best training possible. For his excellent work with people in the armed services, he was recognized as being the black American who had done the most in 1943 to help other black people.

In 1944 Judge Hastie again returned as head of the Howard University Law School. However, it was only a few months before he was called upon to serve his country. Because of his excellent record and ability to understand people, President Harry S. Truman appointed Hastie governor of the Virgin Islands. No black person had ever served as governor of one of our states or an overseas territory. Governor Hastie was well suited for this task. He had done a good job as a judge for the Virgin Islands, and the people trusted and respected him.

In 1949 the Congress of the United States added the Virgin Islands to the Third U. S. Circuit Court of Appeals. To fill the vacancy for a judge of this court, President Truman asked Governor Hastie to be a federal judge of the Third Circuit. Since 1949 Hastie has done his job well and has always been willing to put in the extra hours needed to be a good judge.

Judge Hastie is loved and respected by many people. He has earned that love and respect by his willingness to help others. Each year he selects the top-ranking graduate from a leading law school to work with him for one year as a law clerk. Hastie selects both whites and blacks for this job. The only requirement is that the young student be the best in his or her class and be willing to work hard.

Judge Hastie has had the honor of knowing and working with five United States presidents. He has also been honored by many schools and universities. But Judge Hastie would probably say that his greatest pleasure has come from the knowledge that he has been able to serve humanity and his country.

Reviewing the Story

Fill in each blank with the word or words which completes each sentence correctly.

1. William Hastie graduated from _____ College with honors.

2. Hastie completed his studies in law at _____.

3. After college, William Hastie _____ for two years.

4. Hastie used his legal talents to defend the rights of many _____ Americans.

5. After becoming a lawyer, Hastie began teaching law at _____ in _____.

6. The Secretary of the Interior appointed William Hastie as a _____ _____.

7. In one important case, Hastie worked to protect the rights of the _____ Indians.

8. President _____ appointed William Hastie as judge of the District Court of the Virgin Islands.

Finding Synonyms

Choose the correct synonym and write it in the blank following each word.

rule	stop	finish	take	significant
just	spare	unoccupied	choose	establish

1. prevent _____

6. complete _____

2. accept _____

7. select _____

3. extra _____

8. law _____

4. fair _____

9. vacancy _____

5. important _____

10. organize _____

Understanding the Story

Match the beginning part of each sentence in Column A with its ending in Column B. Write the correct letter of the ending on the blank before each beginning in Column A.

Column A   Column B

1. .... William Hastie was born   a. for two years.

2. .... In 1939 Hastie became the head   b. governor of the Virgin Islands.

3. .... President Harry Truman appointed Hastie   c. in 1904.

4. .... Judge Hastie worked with five   d. from Harvard Law School.

5. .... Before studying law, William Hastie taught   e. presidents of the United States.

6. .... In 1930 Hastie graduated   f. of Howard University Law School.

Patrick Francis Healy

PRESIDENT OF GEORGETOWN UNIVERSITY

In 1873 Patrick Francis Healy became the first black person to serve as president of a major predominantly white university in the United States. In that year he was named president of Georgetown University.

Patrick Healy was born near Macon, Georgia, on February 27, 1834. His father was an Irish planter and his mother a former slave. He had nine brothers and sisters. Patrick's father was determined that the children would be educated and lead free lives. Mr. Healy sent Patrick and the older children to Flushing Quaker School in Long Island, New York. Patrick did not realize when he left that he would never again return to his home. After completing his work at Flushing School, he entered Holy Cross College. By graduation, Patrick had decided to become a Jesuit priest.

Patrick Healy entered the Jesuit Novitiate in Maryland. After graduation, he taught at St. Joseph's College in Philadelphia and at Holy Cross College. After several years of teaching, Patrick attended Georgetown University and also studied at the University of Louvain in Belgium. He was ordained to the priesthood in 1864 and received his Doctor of Philosophy degree the following year. It is believed that Father Patrick Healy was the first black American to receive such a degree.

Father Healy returned to Georgetown University, this time to teach. Because of his wide educational background and teaching ability, he soon became dean of studies. In 1873 he became acting president, and in 1874 he was confirmed as Georgetown University's twenty-ninth president.

Father Healy was very popular with the students, and they welcomed the new changes he brought to the school. During the years Father Healy served as president, he improved the curriculum, reorganized the medical and law schools, and organized an alumni association. Under his guidance, there was constructed a huge building with administration, classroom, and dormitory facilities. It is known today as the Healy Building.

Father Patrick Healy worked extremely

hard as president of Georgetown University, but his health began to fail. He reluctantly retired from his office in 1882 to try to regain his health. However, when Georgetown University celebrated its centennial year in 1889, he was too ill to speak at the ceremonies. Father Healy's last brief assignment was as spiritual father at St. Joseph's College in Philadelphia. As his condition worsened during 1908, he became a patient in the infirmary at Georgetown University. He died there in 1910 and was buried in the campus graveyard, only a short distance from the building bearing his name. Father Healy became known as "the second founder" of Georgetown University because of his many achievements.

Father Patrick Healy's brothers and sisters also made worthwhile individual achievements during their lives. His oldest brother, James Augustine Healy, became the first black Catholic bishop in America. Alexander Sherwood Healy became a distinguished Boston priest. Patrick's sister, Eliza Healy, became a nun and later superior of her Order. And a younger brother, Michael Healy, traveled to Alaska to help the Eskimos and to rescue ships that were in trouble in the arctic waters.

Understanding the Story

Answer the following questions and statements by using the information given in the story.

1. What did Patrick do just after graduating from Holy Cross College? _____

_____

_____

2. Name the first two schools where Patrick Healy taught. _____

_____

3. In what country is the University of Louvain? _____

4. What kind of work did Patrick's father do? _____

_____

5. In what year did Father Healy receive his doctor's degree? _____

6. Name three major things Father Patrick Healy did while serving as president of

   Georgetown University. _____

_____

_____

7. In what year did Father Healy become president of Georgetown University, and in what year did he retire? _____ _____

8. Where is Father Healy buried? _____

_____

Finding the Meanings

Match each word in Column A with its meaning in Column B. Write the correct letter of the meaning on the blank before each word in Column A.

	Column A		Column B
1.	_____ determined	a.	the period of trial and preparation of a new person in a religious order
2.	_____ ordain	b.	a course of study offered at a school
3.	_____ novitiate	c.	a place for the care of the sick or injured in a school
4.	_____ dean	d.	having a fixed purpose
5.	_____ confirm	e.	a building providing sleeping and living accommodations
6.	_____ curriculum	f.	to appoint officially as a member of the clergy
7.	_____ dormitory	g.	a faculty member of a college or university who has special charge of the students
8.	_____ reluctant	h.	showing unwillingness
9.	_____ centennial	i.	to render valid by formal approval
10.	_____ infirmary	j.	having to do with 100 years or the 100th anniversary

Matthew A. Henson

POLAR EXPLORER

It was twenty-five degrees below zero. The cold air burned their lungs, and it was difficult for them to breathe. Ice coated their beards. But they had reached their goal at last. Matthew Henson and Robert Peary were on top of the world. After eighteen hard years and several failures, they had finally made it. They had reached the North Pole.

There was nothing but ice and cold winds at the North Pole on April 6, 1909. But it was a beautiful sight for these two men who had worked so hard for so long to get there. Peary gave Henson an American flag. Peary had kept it wrapped around his body next to his skin. Matthew Henson planted the Stars and Stripes at the North Pole—a place where there is no east, no west, no north, but only south.

Matthew Henson was born in Charles County, Maryland, on August 8, 1866. His mother and father died when he was a young boy. He went to live with his aunt. She was unkind to him, so he left home.

Matthew went to Washington, D. C. and got a job washing dishes in a small restaurant. He didn't stay there long. He had always dreamed of being a sailor, and at the age of thirteen he made up his mind to go to sea. Matthew hiked to the city of Baltimore and walked along the docks. He met the captain of one of the ships, *Katie Hines*. They became friends, and Captain Childs made Matthew a cabin boy. He taught him reading, writing, and arithmetic. He also taught Matthew about the sea and how to pilot a ship. But after five years Captain Childs died, and Matthew Henson left the *Katie*.

Henson again began to look for something to do. He found work in a clothing store. In the spring of 1887 Robert E. Peary, an engineer for the United States Navy, came into the store to buy a helmet. He was going to Nicaragua, a country in Central America. Peary liked Henson and asked him to go with him as his helper. Henson agreed to go. He would have done almost anything to travel and be at sea again.

Peary and Henson were in Nicaragua for only one year. When they returned to the United States, Henson worked as a messenger in Peary's office at the Navy Yard in Philadelphia. After a year, Peary planned a trip to Greenland. He wanted to explore the northern ice cap. Peary could not offer Henson any pay for the trip, but Henson again wanted to go. He later said, "I couldn't spend money up there anyway."

Many people laughed at Peary for taking Henson to the Arctic. They said, "A black man cannot stand the cold as well as a white man." Henson proved that they were wrong.

Henson made seven voyages with Peary to the north country. On the first trip Peary broke his leg, and Henson became the leader of the party.

Because Henson's skin was dark, the Eskimos thought he was one of them. They believed he was an Eskimo who had not learned to talk their language. They thought he had learned to speak only the English language.

The Eskimos taught Henson how to build a sled and to handle a dog team. They taught him to hunt seal, bear, and musk ox. He soon learned to speak the Eskimo language. Henson began to dress like the Eskimos. He wore a fur shirt next to his skin and a hood made of deerskin. He wore trousers made of bearskin and a fold of bearskin around his face. His boots were made of sealskin.

When Peary's leg healed, Henson taught him all he had learned from the Eskimos. He also taught the rest of the party of explorers useful secrets about the frozen North. Henson became the most valuable person in the group. Peary's group could never have reached the North Pole without the help of the Eskimos.

Peary and Henson kept trying to reach the North Pole for many years. Between trips they had to work to raise money for these expeditions. Before each trip

Peary would say to Henson, "We are going back to the Arctic again—but this time, all the way to the North Pole." Each trip seemed harder and harder. Many times they would make camp during the coldest part of the winter and move forward in the spring. Some of the explorers left the expedition and returned to the United States because of the unbearably cold weather. Sometimes they were lost in the blinding blizzards.

Once Peary and his party ran out of food and had to kill their dogs one by one to feed the other dogs and themselves. At one time Peary's feet froze, and he lost eight of his toes. Henson bathed Peary's feet in the snow. He then warmed them against his own stomach, as the Eskimos had taught him to do. But Henson could not save the frozen toes. Although the loss of the toes crippled Peary, he was more determined than ever to reach the North Pole.

Henson was also determined to reach the North Pole. Even though he married in 1907 and started building a house, Henson could not resist the call to go with Peary when he left the United States on his last trip to the North Pole.

Peary and Henson began their last journey with four other Americans and nineteen Eskimos. Along the way, many of the people left the party. When Peary and Henson were about one hundred and thirty miles from the North Pole, they were left with only four Eskimos, five sleds, and a group of husky dogs.

Never before in the history of America have two people, one white and one black, been so dedicated to achieving the same goal. Peary and Henson would not give up.

Danger was always with them, but they pushed on. On the last part of the journey, Henson led the way. Peary rode in one of the sleds because of his crippled feet. Henson built igloos at various points along the way so that they could rest and be out of the blowing wind.

On April 6, 1909, Henson and one of the Eskimos built the last igloo. They had reached the North Pole.

As Peary looked out over the white surface, he said, "This scene my eyes will never see again. Plant the Stars and Stripes over there, Matt, at the North Pole." Matthew Henson planted the American flag at the very top of the earth, bringing honor to the United States of America.

Matthew Henson and Robert E. Peary were very brave. They were truly great explorers. But most of all they were two people that all Americans can be proud of.

Finding Synonyms

Match each word in Column A with its synonym in Column B. Write the correct letter of the synonym on the blank before each word in Column A.

Column A

1. _____ goal
2. _____ several
3. _____ unkind
4. _____ docks
5. _____ unbearable
6. _____ explore
7. _____ blizzard
8. _____ danger

Column B

a. cruel
b. snowstorm
c. piers
d. examine
e. aim
f. some
g. risk
h. intolerable

Reviewing the Story

Underline the word or group of words which completes each sentence correctly.

1. Matthew Henson was born in   (a) Washington, D.C.   (b) Maryland   (c) New York .

2. Matthew always wanted to be a   (a) writer   (b) ship builder   (c) sailor .

3. Henson made   (a) nine   (b) seven   (c) five   voyages with Robert Peary to the frozen north country.

4. It took **(a) many years** **(b) several years** **(c) only a few years** for Peary and Henson to reach the North Pole.

5. On the last long journey, there were **(a) six** **(b) ten** **(c) four** other Americans traveling with Peary and Henson.

6. Peary and Henson arrived at the North Pole in **(a) 1912** **(b) 1908** **(c) 1909** .

7. **(a) All of the people** **(b) One person** **(c) Several people** traveling in the party arrived at the North Pole.

8. **(a) Robert Peary** **(b) Matthew Henson** **(c) One of the Eskimos** planted the American flag at the North Pole.

9. There were a total of **(a) twenty** **(b) sixteen** **(c) twenty-five** people in the party that set out on the last trip to the North Pole.

10. Henson built **(a) igloos** **(b) tents** **(c) brick houses** in which the travelers could rest.

Understanding the Story

Write <u>true</u> or <u>false</u> before each of the following statements.

1. _____ It took Peary and Henson eighteen years to reach the North Pole.

2. _____ Matthew Henson decided to go to sea when he was nine years old.

3. _____ Nicaragua is a country in Central America.

4. _____ On the first trip with Peary, Matthew Henson broke his leg.

5. _____ The Eskimos acted unfriendly toward Henson and Peary.

6. _____ Peary and Henson were brave explorers from the United States.

7. _____ The Eskimos thought Henson was one of them.

8. _____ After 1907, Henson stayed at home and did not travel with Robert Peary.

Mahalia Jackson

GOSPEL SINGER

Only a grand person like Mahalia Jackson could have been loved and admired by so many people. She was probably the world's greatest gospel singer. Her broad smile and rhythmic bounce charmed millions of people. Wherever she went, there were cheering crowds to greet her. Millions of people—men and women of all races, poor and rich, those with musical training and those without musical training—enjoyed the style of music that she knew best.

This little orphan girl from New Orleans, Louisiana, came a long way. When she was born on October 26, 1911, there was little chance that she might someday become a great star.

Mahalia Jackson spent the early days of her childhood on the rough New Orleans waterfront. Her mother, Charity Jackson, died when Mahalia was very young. Her father, John Andrew Jackson, died when she was six years old. Before his death Mr. Jackson worked on the docks. At night he worked as a barber, and on Sundays he was a preacher in a small church. Mahalia grew up singing many religious songs in the church choir.

Mahalia was a very unhappy little girl who was left alone most of the time. She was washing and ironing for several families before she was ten. Too busy to have any fun, the only real happiness she had was singing in her church choir.

Mahalia left New Orleans and went to Chicago when she was sixteen years old. She was looking for something to do with her life. She had hopes of studying beauty culture or nursing. But to take care of herself she got a job in a Chicago factory. She earned only a little more than one dollar a day. She also took part-time jobs scrubbing floors and curling hair.

Working with the church was always a very important part of Mahalia Jackson's life. During her first week in Chicago, she joined a church and began singing in the church choir. The director of the choir formed a special group with Mahalia as the main soloist. The church choir was asked to sing at revivals and other church programs.

Mahalia's real boost into fame came

in 1945 when she made a recording of "Move on Up a Little Higher." This record became a best seller and sold over a million copies. It was a religious song, but jazz fans liked its catchy rhythm. When her record reached Europe, Mahalia Jackson was hailed as a great new American artist.

In the United States, booking agents began to look for this singer who had suddenly become so famous. They wanted to know who she was and where she was. Many people wanted to hear this new star. She had to move her concerts from churches to larger auditoriums. Crowds wanted to hear her "modern" religious songs.

Mahalia Jackson became one of the busiest singers of the day. She was invited to give a concert in Carnegie Hall in New York City. Only great artists are invited to appear in this great hall. All seats were sold. When she gave her second concert there, hundreds of people were turned away. The same thing happened when she went to Denmark, France, and England. Her new art, gospel singing, had become a favorite of music lovers.

Since Mahalia Jackson never had a music lesson, she could not read musical notes and almost never sang a song the same way twice. When she opened her mouth, music just seemed to pour out with a kind of charming power.

"What did this singer have that earned her the honor of being invited to give concerts in a place like Carnegie Hall?" some have questioned. Although her music spoke for itself, Mahalia tried to answer such questions. She said that she sang what she felt deep inside her. She enjoyed singing as much as her audience enjoyed hearing her. She once said, "When I sing at concerts, sometimes I whisper. Sometimes I exclaim and drive the rhythm real hard. Sometimes I get right down off the stage and get down on my knees and sing with the folk. Sometimes I keep right on singing in my dressing room before I've sung all that I feel inside me."

Mahalia Jackson's singing seemed to have a strong effect upon the listener. The person who heard her once usually wanted to hear her again and again. She was a gospel singer for over thirty years and always seemed to draw more fans wherever she went.

Mahalia Jackson was deeply religious, and she showed it in her work. She sang her songs of faith in churches, concert halls, radio and television studios, baseball parks, arenas, and many other such places. She also had the honor of being invited to sing at the White House.

Because her singing was so attractive to the general public, Mahalia had many offers to sing in bars and nightclubs. No amount of money, no matter how great, was able to tempt her. She said that she could not sing spirituals about the Lord in those places.

Mahalia was a "big" person. She was not only big in size but big in other ways, too. She always seemed to have a big smile. She had a big beautiful voice, and she had a big heart. She gave much of her time and money to help others who were in need. Mahalia Jackson said that her willingness to help others was a way to express "the happiness and strength that can come from the Lord."

Understanding the Story

Match the beginning part of each sentence in Column A with its ending in Column B.
Write the correct letter of the ending on the blank before each beginning in Column A.

Column A

Column B

1. _____ Mahalia Jackson was a great

a. when she was six years old.

2. _____ Mahalia was born

b. a music lesson in her life.

3. _____ As a child, Mahalia began singing

c. a record that sold over a million copies.

4. _____ When Mahalia was sixteen years old, she moved

d. and always tried to help other people.

5. _____ Mahalia Jackson became famous in 1945 when she made

e. gospel singer.

6. _____ Mahalia gave concerts

f. in New York City.

7. _____ Mahalia never had

g. to Chicago.

8. _____ Carnegie Hall is

h. in Carnegie Hall.

9. _____ Mahalia had a big heart

i. in New Orleans.

10. _____ Mahalia became an orphan

j. in the church choir.

Reviewing the Story

Underline the word or group of words which completes each sentence correctly.

1. Mahalia Jackson was born in the year **(a) 1906** **(b) 1915** **(c) 1911** .

2. In **(a) 1950** **(b) 1945** **(c) 1940** Mahalia Jackson was hailed as a great new American artist after she recorded a religious song called "Move on Up a Little Higher."

3. Mahalia had a very **(a) happy** **(b) unhappy** childhood.

4. Throughout her many years of singing, Mahalia Jackson never accepted invitations to sing in **(a) churches** **(b) nightclubs** **(c) concert halls** .

Finding Synonyms

Match each word in Column A with its synonym in Column B. Write the correct letter of the synonym on the blank before each word in Column A.

Column A

1. _____ grand
2. _____ charm
3. _____ dock
4. _____ factory
5. _____ director
6. _____ boost
7. _____ fame
8. _____ usual
9. _____ audience
10. _____ sudden

Column B

a. plant

b. listeners

c. splendid

d. unexpected

e. wharf

f. prominence

g. leader

h. delight

i. ordinary

j. lift

William H. Johnson

ARTIST

As a black child born in 1901 in Florence, South Carolina, William Henry Johnson could expect a life of poverty and hard work in the cotton fields. Yet William dreamed of a different future. He wanted to become an artist.

As a child William worked odd jobs to help feed his mother and younger siblings. When he was only 17, he left Florence for New York City, where he hoped to study art. In New York William cooked and carried bags at hotels and loaded ships on the docks. In 1921 he was accepted at the National Academy of Design. William was an excellent student.

During the summers William studied with a painter named George Hawthorne. Hawthorne provided money to send William to Paris, France, to study. William experimented with painting in the style of French artists of the time. An art gallery in Paris held the first one-person show of Johnson's work.

In 1929 William Johnson met a Dutch woman named Holcha Krake. She was an artist who made pottery and cloth.

Together they traveled through Europe. Johnson tried painting in the different styles that were popular in Europe. He was good at all of them, but he had not yet found a style of his own.

In 1930 Johnson returned to New York. He entered some of his paintings in a contest held by the Harmon Foundation, whose goal was to help black artists. William won first prize! During this time he visited briefly his hometown in South Carolina. But William was soon ready to return to Europe, where people could accept the idea of a black artist more easily.

Johnson married Holcha Krake, and they settled in a Danish fishing village. William understood the hardworking people of the little town. He and Holcha traveled in Denmark and Norway, where many people were eager to buy his paintings. However, the paintings Johnson sent back to the Harmon Foundation in the U.S. did not sell.

In 1932 William and Holcha traveled to Germany, France, and Tunisia. In Tunisia they learned about African arts and crafts. They learned about how the people of Tunisia lived. At that time Europeans were interested in folk culture. It was this interest that may have caused Johnson to see his past in South Carolina with new eyes.

William and Holcha's comfortable life in Denmark soon came to an end. In 1938 it was clear that there would be a war in Europe. Johnson was afraid that Denmark would be taken over by the fascists in Germany. He and Holcha moved to New York.

Once again Johnson's style of painting changed. He began to paint in a primitive, folk art style, with rough, powerful forms and bright colors. Also, for the first time, his paintings showed the lives of black people. He painted the people of Harlem and scenes from his childhood in South Carolina. Johnson had found his own style at last.

In 1943 disaster struck. First William's apartment burned. Only a few months later Holcha died of cancer. William soon became sick with a brain disorder. He could not care for himself, and he was sent to live in a mental hospital in New York State. William Johnson never painted again. He died in the hospital in 1970.

Luckily, the Harmon Foundation saved William's paintings. Today people in America have become more interested in his work. In 1992 two exhibitions were held in New York. Many people came to see William's vivid and moving images of black Americans. At last William Johnson had found recognition in his own country.

Understanding the Story

Write true or false before each of the following statements.

1. _____ William left Florence for New York City when he was 17.

2. _____ In New York William worked as a bus driver.

3. _____ William was an outstanding student at the National Academy of Design.

4. _____ William won first prize in a contest held by the Harmon Foundation.

5. _____ Johnson and his wife made their first home in New Jersey.

6. _____ Johnson couldn't understand the people in the Danish fishing village where he lived.

7. _____ Many people in the U.S. were eager to buy the paintings Johnson sent to the Harmon Foundation.

8. _____ In Tunisia William and Holcha learned about African arts and crafts.

9. _____ William and Holcha moved from Denmark to New York to be closer to William's family.

10. ----------------- Johnson showed the lives of black people in his paintings.

11. ----------------- Johnson was sent to live in a mental hospital because he could no longer care for himself.

12. -----------------Johnson completed many paintings in the mental hospital.

Finding Antonyms

Choose the correct antonym and write it in the blank following each word.

weak   lazy   bored   healthy

poor   peace   dark   future

1. powerful   -----------------

2. excellent   -----------------

3. hardworking   -----------------

4. ill   -----------------

5. interested   -----------------

6. bright   -----------------

7. past   -----------------

8. war   -----------------

Barbara Jordan

UNITED STATES REPRESENTATIVE

In November 1972 Barbara Jordan was elected as United States Representative from Houston, Texas, and she became the first black woman elected to Congress from the South. Barbara Jordan has held so many "firsts" that it seemed inevitable that she would win the election.

Barbara Jordan was born on February 21, 1936, in Houston, Texas. She grew up and went to school in Houston. After graduating from high school in the upper five percent of her class, she obtained her degree in political science and history from Texas Southern University, graduating with high honors.

After college Barbara Jordan wanted to become a lawyer. She attended Boston University School of Law and graduated in 1959. She made use of her teaching talents and taught political science at Tuskegee Institute in Alabama. She also practiced law in Houston.

Barbara Jordan worked for a year as administrative assistant to the county judge of Harris County, Texas, before being elected to the Texas senate in 1966. She was the first black woman to serve in the Texas senate. She was re-elected and served until 1972. When the legislature convened for a special session in 1972, Barbara Jordan was unanimously elected president *pro tempore* of the senate and was the first black woman to preside over a state senate. She was also honored by being chosen "Governor for a Day," and she became the first black woman to serve as governor in the history of the United States.

Barbara Jordan was an energetic and able member of the Texas senate and served on many of the major committees. She concentrated on bills to extend workers' compensation benefits, to give Texas its first minimum-wage law, and to establish a department for community affairs designed to solve the problems of urban minorities.

While serving as a state senator, she was one of five people named to the Texas Legislative Council. She was the only first-term senator ever to serve on this important council.

Barbara Jordan was a delegate to the Democratic National Convention in 1968 and was a member of the Executive Committee of the Democratic Policy Council. At the 1970 Texas State Democratic Convention, she was appointed permanent secretary.

Because of Barbara Jordan's dynamic work in politics, Texans on Capitol Hill were predicting, about a year before the 1972 elections, that she would run for and win election to the United States House of Representatives. She won the election and became the only woman member of the 26 member Texas delegation in the United States House of Representatives. Representative Jordan became nationally known through her work. She was one of the most highly publicized members of the House Judiciary Committee that recommended, after lengthy national televised hearings, that President Nixon be impeached and removed from office.

Barbara Jordan served in the House of Representatives for six years. In 1978 she resigned from office and returned to teaching. Barbara Jordan holds the Lyndon Johnson Chair in National Policy at the Lyndon B. Johnson School of Public Affairs of the University of Texas at Austin. She continues to be active in politics. In 1991 Jordan was named special counsel on ethics to the governor of Texas, Ann Richards. She was the keynote speaker at the 1992 Democratic National Convention.

Barbara Jordan has been given many honors and awards. She was selected by United Press International as one of the top ten most influential women in Texas. Barbara Jordan continues to use her talents for the good of the people.

Understanding the Story

Answer the following questions and statements by using information given in the story.

1. At what school did Representative Jordan study law? _____

_____

2. Name three of the "firsts" that Barbara Jordan has held during her political

career. _____

_____

_____

3. What special recognition did U.S. Representative Barbara Jordan receive from

United Press International? _____

_____

4. Name the committee in the House of Representatives that is responsible for conducting hearings on the possible impeachment of a president. _____

_____

5. Why did many members of Congress predict that Barbara Jordan would win election to the House of Representatives? _____

_____

6. At what school did Barbara Jordan teach political science? _____

_____

Finding the Meanings

Match each word in Column A with its meaning in Column B. Write the correct letter of the meaning on the blank before each word in Column A.

Column A	Column B
1. _____ inevitable	a. without a single opposing vote
2. _____ talent	b. intended to last
3. _____ convene	c. to pay close attention
4. _____ unanimously	d. a special natural ability
5. _____ preside	e. to bring to the attention of the public
6. _____ concentrate	f. to tell beforehand
7. _____ permanent	g. not to be avoided
8. _____ publicize	h. to meet for some purpose
9. _____ dynamic	i. to hold the place of authority
10. _____ predict	j. energetic or forceful

Martin Luther King, Jr.

MINISTER AND CIVIL RIGHTS LEADER

Martin Luther King, winner of the Nobel Peace Prize, worked to bring about equality for black people by peaceful means. From 1955 to 1965, Dr. King's nonviolent pleas for racial justice were most successful. His eloquent speeches, in which he expressed his hopes of leading black people to a better and equal life, won the support of millions of people.

King was born on January 15, 1929, in Atlanta, Georgia. His mother was a teacher and his father a minister. Martin graduated from high school at the age of fifteen after skipping two grades. He attended Morehouse College and received his degree in 1948.

It was during college that he decided to enter the ministry. He was ordained a minister in his father's church in Atlanta in 1947 and became assistant pastor. Martin went to Crozer Theological Seminary and Boston University for advanced studies. He was awarded a doctor's degree in theology in 1955.

In 1953 Martin Luther King married Coretta Scott. He became pastor of the Dexter Avenue Baptist Church in Montgomery, Alabama, in 1954. The following year, he actively began his civil rights crusade. He encouraged the people to register to vote and to join the N.A.A.C.P. Dr. King successfully led a boycott of buses in Montgomery, Alabama, to protest the segregation of black passengers, and in 1956 the Supreme Court upheld the desegregation of buses. To coordinate the work of civil rights groups, he helped to establish the Southern Christian Leadership Conference in 1957, and he became its president.

Dr. King spoke and traveled throughout the country and led many demonstrations. In 1963, to protest racial discrimination, he led a march in Birmingham, Alabama, and a sit-in demonstration in Florida the following year. His most successful march was in Washington, D. C., during 1963. More than 250,000 people marched from the Washington Monument to the Lincoln Memorial. At the Lincoln Memorial, Dr. King made his famous "I have a Dream" speech. His effective leadership helped influence

Congress to enact the Civil Rights Act of 1964 and the Voting Rights Act of 1965.

By 1965 Dr. King and his followers were faced with difficulties. The war in Vietnam was diverting attention away from civil rights. To encourage unity, he planned a "Poor People's March" on Washington, D. C., for 1968, but he did not live to lead the march.

During the years, Dr. King received many honorary degrees from universities and medals from religious and civic organizations. In 1963 a national magazine chose him "Man of the Year." Perhaps his greatest honor was when he was named the winner of the Nobel Peace Prize in 1964. Dr. King also wrote five books telling of his beliefs and experiences.

Dr. Martin Luther King died at the age of thirty-nine on April 4, 1968. A hidden rifleman shot and killed him in Memphis, Tennessee. Later, James Earl Ray, an escaped convict, pleaded guilty to the crime and was sentenced to prison.

Dr. King is buried near Ebenezer Baptist Church in Atlanta, Georgia. On his tombstone are carved the words: "Free at last, free at last, thank God Almighty, I'm free at last."

Understanding the Story

Write true or false before each of the following statements.

1. _____ Martin Luther King was born during the year 1929.

2. _____ The civil rights movement, led by Dr. King, was most successful from 1940 to 1950.

3. _____ In 1955 Dr. King received a doctor's degree in sociology.

4. _____ Dr. King led a boycott of buses in Montgomery, Alabama.

5. _____ At the Washington Monument, Dr. King made his famous "I Have a Dream" speech.

6. _____ During his life, Martin Luther King wrote three books.

7. _____ Dr. King died in Atlanta, Georgia.

8. _____ An escaped convict confessed to the murder of Dr. King.

9. _____ Dr. King was buried in Atlanta, Georgia.

10. _____ During 1960 Dr. King was chosen "Man of the Year."

11. _____ In 1963 Dr. Martin Luther King led a march in Birmingham, Alabama, to protest racial discrimination.

Finding Synonyms

Match each word in Column A with its synonym in Column B. Write the correct letter of the synonym on the blank before each word in Column A.

Column A

1. _____ plea
2. _____ justice
3. _____ eloquent
4. _____ crusade
5. _____ upheld
6. _____ effective
7. _____ divert
8. _____ influence

Column B

a. campaign

b. distract

c. fairness

d. impressive

e. appeal

f. move

g. expressive

h. supported

Thurgood Marshall

ASSOCIATE JUSTICE, SUPREME COURT OF THE UNITED STATES

In 1967 Thurgood Marshall became the first black justice to serve on the United States Supreme Court. Through this appointment, Justice Marshall reached the highest level in the judicial system of this nation.

The Supreme Court is the highest court of the land. It must decide the outcome of cases in which the decision of a lower court is questioned by a lawyer or the person on trial. When a lower court gives a verdict of "guilty," the person on trial can have his or her lawyers appeal the verdict to a higher court. The appeal must first go to one of the lower state or federal courts. Finally the appeal may go all the way to the top—to the United States Supreme Court.

The Supreme Court has the power to review all the facts in a person's trial and make the final decision about the verdict. The Supreme Court may reverse the decision reached by the lower courts and judge the accused person "not guilty."

The Supreme Court is also called upon to decide cases in which the United States Constitution is questioned.

For example, lower courts for many years upheld laws that required all voters to pay a poll tax. But in March of 1965, the U.S. Supreme Court declared that the poll tax was unconstitutional. As an associate justice of the Supreme Court, Thurgood Marshall had a voice in making such important decisions.

Marshall was born in Baltimore, Maryland. His great-grandfather was a slave, his mother a schoolteacher, and his father a steward in a fashionable club on Chesapeake Bay. Young Marshall was a good student, and at an early age he showed his determination to get an education. He worked his way through Lincoln University as a cafeteria busboy and a dining-car waiter.

After completing his work at Lincoln, he decided to enter law school. He applied for admission to the University of Maryland Law School, only to be told that he could not attend the all-white school. However, he did not give up his desire to become a lawyer. He studied law at Howard University in Washington, D.C. His expenses were paid in part by his mother, who pawned her wedding and engagement rings so that he would have money for tuition and books.

He graduated from Howard University Law School in 1933 and returned to Baltimore to set up his practice. He soon became well-known as an able lawyer who handled his cases with honesty and fairness, as well as with a broad knowledge of the law. He successfully presented a case which forced Maryland public schools to pay black teachers a salary equal to other public school teachers of Maryland. Then in 1935 he succeeded in getting the first black person admitted to the University of Maryland Law School, the same school that years before had refused to admit him.

Thurgood Marshall had an opportunity to earn national respect when he was appointed chief legal counsel for the N.A.A.C.P. and its Legal Defense and Educational Fund. He served in this important position for 23 years and established an excellent record as a lawyer. His legal battles for equal rights included 32 cases before the Supreme Court. He won all but three cases.

Marshall's most famous victory was the case of Brown versus the Topeka Board of Education. This case came before the Supreme Court in 1954. It involved the refusal of a school board to admit blacks to the previously all-white public schools in Topeka, Kansas. Thurgood Marshall argued against the schools' refusing black students, and his arguments moved the Supreme Court to decide in favor of ending segregation in public schools.

Although Marshall earned the respect of other lawyers for his ability to handle difficult legal problems, he was also known for his sense of humor and friendly manner. Many stories are told that point out his wit and sense of humor. In 1951 during the Korean

conflict, Marshall went to Korea as a lawyer for forty black people who were accused of committing a crime. After the trial Marshall wanted to visit the battlefront. During his visit he and his escort, Colonel D.D. Martin, were surprised by gunfire. Quickly both men dived for a ditch. When the shooting stopped, Colonel Martin could not see Marshall. He yelled, "Marshall, where are you?" A voice replied, "Are you kidding? Under you!"

As a result of his work with the N.A.A.C.P., Thurgood Marshall's reputation for fairness came to the attention of important government officials. In 1961 President John F. Kennedy appointed Marshall as a federal judge of the U.S. Second Circuit Court of Appeals. This court has authority to hear appeals from New York, Connecticut, and Vermont. As a federal judge, Marshall was an immediate success. His impartial administration of justice showed the same fairness and honesty that had characterized his actions as a lawyer.

Because of his excellent record, Marshall was asked in 1965 by President Johnson to become solicitor general of the United States, one of our government's chief lawyers. So, at the age of 57, Marshall chose to take a cut in salary and give up his lifetime judgeship in order to serve his country where the president felt he was needed. Marshall became the nation's thirty-third solicitor general and the first black to hold the position.

The solicitor general has the responsibility of representing the United States in cases argued before the Supreme Court. He or she must speak for the nation as a whole whenever the federal government is involved in a case.

In his job as associate justice of the Supreme Court, Thurgood Marshall moved from arguing cases to deciding them in the same court. His experience as solicitor general made him familiar with the workings of the Supreme Court. His experience as a successful lawyer and a respected federal judge gave him the habit of demanding truth and justice for all.

Thurgood Marshall served as a member of the Supreme Court until his retirement in 1991. When Justice Marshall died on January 24, 1993, the nation mourned the loss of this great man. As a lawyer, judge, and Supreme Court justice Thurgood Marshall played a crucial role in securing many of the rights that Americans of all races now enjoy.

Reviewing the Story

Fill in each blank with the word or group of words which completes each sentence correctly.

1. In 1967 Thurgood Marshall was appointed _____ of the Supreme Court.

2. The _____ is the highest court in the United States.

3. Marshall studied law at _____.

4. After graduating from law school, Marshall set up his law practice in the city of _____.

5. Thurgood Marshall was appointed chief legal counsel for the _____ _____.

6. Marshall's most famous legal case involved the segregation of public schools in _____.

7. The case of Brown versus the Topeka Board of Education led to the ending of _____ in public schools.

8. In 1961 Marshall became a _____.

9. The Supreme Court may _____ a decision made by a lower court.

10. In 1965 President Johnson asked Marshall to become _____ of the United States.

11. While serving as solicitor general, Thurgood Marshall represented the United States in cases argued before the _____.

Finding Antonyms

Choose the correct antonym and write it in the blank following each word.

higher	innocent	failure	slow
beginning	biased	allow	part

1. impartial ---------------------------

2. guilty ---------------------------

3. whole ---------------------------

4. lower ---------------------------

5. success ---------------------------

6. quick ---------------------------

7. final ---------------------------

8. refuse ---------------------------

Jan Ernst Matzeliger

INVENTOR

Jan Matzeliger completely changed the art of making shoes when he invented the first shoemaking machine. Born on September 15, 1852, in a small country on the northern coast of South America, Jan Matzeliger was a foreign-born black who came to the United States.

When Jan was a small boy, his father, an engineer, taught him about machines. By the time he was ten years old, Jan was working in a machine shop.

Jan was still quite young when his family moved to America. They first settled in Philadelphia, Pennsylvania, where Jan learned to be a shoemaker. Later the Matzeliger family moved to Lynn, Massachusetts, where Jan found work in a shoe factory.

Making shoes during that time was a very hard and slow job. There were no machines, and every operation had to be done by hand. Sitting on a bench and bending over shoes all day meant hard work for any cobbler. It took many hours just to make one shoe.

The process and conditions under which Jan Matzeliger had to work started

him thinking. In 1877 he began to experiment with ideas about how to invent a machine for making shoes. He rented a room over an old church and began his work on a project that would take him many years.

Matzeliger's task was a very difficult one. He had many problems and handicaps. His greatest problem was finding time to build his machine. Since he had to work long hours at the shoe factory, he did not have very much time to work on his machine. He also lacked the money to buy many of the materials for his experiments.

Even though there were so many things in his way, Matzeliger slowly began to build his machine. He often became discouraged, but he had one thing in his favor—he believed in himself. He never doubted that one day his work would end in success. So he worked on, slowly solving first one problem and then another.

Matzeliger had to make his own equipment from homemade tools. He made models of his plans out of scraps of wood and cigar boxes. When one thing would not work, he tried another. He felt that each attempt was a step in the right direction.

Finally Matzeliger built a model that seemed to be what he wanted. He used an old forge to make the moving parts. He shaped the gears and wheels and put them into place. How happy and excited he was when the model worked! His dream had been realized.

The machine was a great success. The difficult job of hand pleating the leather and fitting the upper part of the shoes to the soles was no longer necessary. Matzeliger had made a machine that would hold the shoe on the last, grip and pull the leather down around the heel, and then drive the nails into place. With this machine, a cobbler could make a shoe in less than half the time that had been needed before.

Jan Matzeliger's machine soon made Lynn, Massachusetts, the shoe capital of the world. The patent for the machine was sold to the United Shoe Machinery Company. The company soon was worth millions of dollars.

Many people were helped by this invention. The shoe industry was once limited to only a few skilled workers. With the invention of the shoe-lasting machine, thousands of new jobs were created. Many people were needed to operate the machines of the rapidly growing shoe industry.

Many people were helped in another way, too. Since the machine greatly reduced the time required to make a pair of shoes, the cost of labor was not as great. The price of a pair of shoes was cut in half. At the same time, wages for the operators of machines were doubled. Factory conditions were improved, and the drudgery of long, back-breaking hours in making shoes was no longer necessary. In a very short time the number of shoes exported from the United States increased from one million to over eleven million pairs a year.

Today a Matzeliger-type machine can be found in nearly every shoe factory of the modern world. Jan Matzeliger did not live to see the great good that he had done. He did not make a lot of money from his invention, but he left an enduring monument to the good he did for humanity.

Understanding the Story

Write true or false before each of the following statements.

1. _____ Jan Matzeliger invented the first shoemaking machine.

2. _____ Jan lived during the 1700s.

3. _____ Jan was born in a small country in Europe.

4. _____ It took Matzeliger many years to complete his invention.

5. _____ Because of the machine, the price of a pair of shoes was doubled.

6. _____ When the shoe-lasting machine was invented, many new jobs were created.

7. _____ Jan Matzeliger made a great deal of money from his invention.

8. _____ Jan's father was an engineer.

9. _____ Matzeliger did not believe that he would ever successfully finish a shoemaking machine.

10. _____ Jan learned to be a shoemaker in New York City.

Finding Antonyms

Choose the correct antonymn and write it in the blank following each word.

import	elderly	quick	lose	bought
inland	stay	easy	failure	long

1. move _____

2. short _____

3. coast _____

4. find _____

5. sold _____

6. difficult _____

7. export _____

8. slow _____

9. success _____

10. young _____

Willie Mays

BASEBALL STAR

One day in the summer of 1941, two small boys were playing catch in a vacant lot in Fairfield, Alabama. One of the boys was Willie Mays. The other was Willie's best friend, Charles Willis. As they happily threw the ball to each other, Willie Mays said, "Hey, Charles, call me DiMaggio. Maybe one day I'll be great like him!"

Willie was only ten years old then, and Joe DiMaggio was his idol. To Willie, Di-Maggio was as great a baseball player as anyone could be—maybe even better than Babe Ruth.

Willie had a love for sports even before he had heard of Joe DiMaggio. Some people have said that he was "born to play baseball." He was born into a family of athletes. His father was a fine outfielder, and his grandfather was a good pitcher. His mother had been a star in track. Before Willie could walk, he enjoyed the game of rolling a ball to his father. When they would stop playing, Willie would cry. Since those early days. Willie Mays and his father have continued to be very close. They have

not only been father and son but very good friends as well.

Willie and his father have always spent a lot of time together. When Willie was two years old, his parents were divorced. His mother remarried, and Willie was left in the care of his father and Aunt Sarah. His father never married again and spent most of his evenings with his son. Willie and his father talked about many things but mostly about sports.

Mr. Mays talked more about baseball than any other sport. He worked in a steel mill and played on the company baseball team. Willie loved to go out to the ballpark and watch his father play. During the day Willie played sandlot baseball and practiced what he had learned from his father.

Soon Willie had learned to catch, throw, run, and hit as well as anyone on his father's team. But Mr. Mays kept saying, "Willie, practice picking the ball up. You must practice some plays more than others. Learning to pick up a hard-hit ground ball is one of the hardest plays."

Willie followed his father's advice. He practiced very hard. The two of them often played a baseball warm-up game. Mr. Mays watched for mistakes and helped Willie correct them.

Willie Mays loved other sports, too. In high school he was a triple-threat halfback in football. He was a great passer, kicker, and runner. He was even better in basketball. When he was sixteen, he led the county in scoring. He played each sport the same way he played baseball—as if he could see in every direction at once. His remarkable talent for being aware of everything around him helped Willie Mays to become a super star.

Since his high school did not have a baseball team, Willie could play only sandlot ball. At first Willie wanted to be a pitcher. However, he soon changed his mind. One day, while pitching a game in very hot weather, Willie fainted. He just put too much energy into his pitching. His father talked him into playing in the outfield. "At least outfielders get to play every day," Mr. Mays said. "Pitchers don't." Willie soon realized that he could help his team more by playing every game in the outfield.

Willie's father helped him get a break in professional baseball. He introduced him to Piper Davis, the manager of the Birmingham Black Barons. This was one of the best teams in the Negro National League. Willie Mays got a job as an extra player for the summer when he was only sixteen. Willie did so well that he became a regular member of the team. In fact, a major league team tried to sign him up, but Mr. Mays would not let Willie sign up because he had not finished high school. Even though Willie had a chance to make a lot of money by dropping out of school and playing baseball, Mr. Mays knew that Willie's education had to come first.

When Willie did finish high school, he got his chance of a lifetime. He was signed by the New York Giants. When the scout for the Giants saw Willie play, he said, "My eyes almost popped out of my head when I saw that young boy swing the bat with such speed and power. He is the greatest young ballplayer I have ever seen."

The scout for the Giants had to work fast. Other scouts were watching Willie, too. The next morning the scout talked to Willie. Willie had no contract with the Black Barons, so he told the scout to deal with his father and Aunt Sarah.

They all met at Willie's house that afternoon. How proud they were when Willie signed his first contract! Mr. Mays retired from baseball for good. "One baseball player in the family is enough," he said. Although Willie was not under contract with the Birmingham team, the Giants gave the Black Barons' owner $10,000 for letting Willie leave his team.

Willie was sent to the Giants' training farm in New Jersey. He batted well and made surprising catches. The next year he moved up to their Minneapolis team. He liked what he was doing. He played hard and had fun doing it. Willie Mays listened to his coaches, and he watched the other players. He was eager to learn from others, and he knew they could teach him how to play better.

The 1951 season was a bad one for the Giants. They began with a losing streak of eleven games. While the Giants were losing in New York, Willie was going great in Minneapolis. Leo Durocher, the manager of the Giants, decided to call Willie. He had watched Willie play in spring training in Florida and had liked the way Willie played.

Willie was watching a movie when he heard his name called over the public address system. He was told to return to his hotel. Once back at the hotel, he was told to call Mr. Durocher. "What for?" Mays asked. "The big league wants you," he was told. "Not me—I'm not ready," Willie said. Durocher would not take no for an answer, so Willie joined the Giants major league team.

Willie Mays had a hard time getting started. He failed to get a hit his first two days with the Giants. But the Giants were winning again. Durocher said that Mays must have been what the team needed. The team needed a spark of inspiration. Maybe they wanted to show their "new rookie star" what they could do.

After three games, Willie Mays finally got a hit—a home run. By the end of the season Mays was selected as "Rookie of the Year" for 1951. He was a great fielder. He made catches that were unbelievable. His throws seemed impossible.

From that day on, life for Willie was not the same. The game of baseball was not the same, either. He was only nineteen, but he became one of the greatest players of all time. Never before had a ballplayer had so much life! His happy-go-lucky manner won him many friends. Willie spoke to everyone, but he had trouble remembering names, so he greeted everyone by saying, "Say Hey." Willie Mays soon became known as the "Say Hey Kid."

After starting the 1952 season, Mays was drafted into the United States Army. He didn't mind, for he was only twenty-one at that time. He said it was better to be drafted young instead of in the middle of a baseball career. He also knew that he had a duty and a responsibility to his country.

While playing baseball in the army, Mays worked out his famous breadbasket catch. It became his trademark. By catching the ball at his waist, he felt that he could save time in throwing the ball.

When he returned home in 1954, the Giants again won the pennant and the World Series. At the end of the season Mays was named Most Valuable Player in the National League. He was also selected as the Major League Player of 1954. Eleven years later and after the Giants had moved to San Francisco, Willie Mays again was named the National League's Most Valuable Player.

In 1972 Willie Mays was traded to the New York Mets. He played his last years of professional baseball in the city where he began his exciting career. Willie quit as an active player after the 1973 World Series, but he is still active in baseball. He works with the New York Mets in public relations and as a coach.

Baseball has been good to Willie, and Willie has been good for baseball. He played a clean game and was a showman but not a show-off. He continues to be the idol of many young players. His teammates will long remember his "Say Hey" spirit. The secret of his success has been his love for what he is doing and his constant efforts to improve himself.

Finding the Meanings

Match each word in Column A with its meaning in Column B. Write the correct letter of the meaning on the blank before each word in Column A.

Column A

Column B

1. _____ vacant

a. cannot be or happen

2. _____ advice

b. a formal agreement between two or more parties

3. _____ realize

c. a novice or beginner

4. _____ contract

d. an opinion given as to what should be done

5. _____ retire

e. never stopping

6. _____ rookie

f. empty

7. _____ impossible

g. to understand

8. _____ constant

h. to withdraw oneself from business or active service

9. _____ pitcher

i. extraordinary or unusual

10. _____ remarkable

j. the player who throws the ball to a batter

Reviewing the Story

Fill in each blank with the word or group of words which completes each sentence correctly.

1. As a child, Willie's baseball idol was _____.

2. When Willie's father played baseball, he was an _____.

3. During his high school years, Willie first wanted to be a _____,

   but later he played in the _____.

4. At the age of sixteen, Willie played for the _____

   _____ baseball team during the summer.

5. Mr. Mays wanted Willie to finish _____

   before signing a contract to play major league baseball.

6. Willie Mays began his major league career with the _____

   _____.

7. The first games that Willie played with a major league team was during the

   _____ season.

8. After three games in professional baseball, Willie's first hit was a _____

   _____.

9. Willie Mays was named Most Valuable Player in the National League during the

   _____ and _____ seasons.

10. When Willie caught the baseball at his waist, he was making one of his famous

    _____ catches.

11. After Willie Mays signed his first contract, he was sent to the training farm in

    _____.

12. Willie Mays had trouble remembering names so he said "_____"

    when he greeted everyone.

Constance Baker Motley

UNITED STATES DISTRICT JUDGE

Constance Baker Motley, an attorney and United States district judge, was born on September 14, 1921, in New Haven, Connecticut. She and her brothers and sisters grew up and attended school in New Haven.

A bright student, Constance Baker was usually first or second in her high school class at New Haven High School. She enjoyed playing basketball and also took part in debate. Her low but persuasive voice was of great value to her when speaking before a group.

Constance Baker became very interested in people and events in history and spent much of her free time reading about early black Americans. She became involved in the problems related to civil rights and was elected president of the local N.A.A.C.P. youth council.

At one time, Constance Baker had thought of becoming an interior decorator, but her goals changed. She decided that she wanted to become a lawyer. However, her family did not have the money to send Constance to college. She wanted to work to pay for her college education, but it was very difficult to find a job.

Suddenly her future changed. One evening Constance Baker gave a speech at the Dixwell Community House, a black social center, in which she urged that black people be given greater responsibilities in life. In the audience was Clarence W. Blakeslee, a white businessman and philanthropist. He was so impressed with Constance Baker's honest and sincere manner that he offered to finance her education. She was given her choice of schools, and she decided on Fisk University in Nashville, Tennessee. A year and a half later she transferred to New York University, and in 1943 she earned a degree in economics.

The 1940s were important years for Constance Baker. After completing her work at New York University, she attended Columbia University Law School. While studying law, she began working as a clerk on the legal staff of the N.A.A.C.P. Legal and Educational Defense Fund which was headed by Thurgood Marshall.

In 1946 Constance Baker married Joel Wilson Motley who was studying law at New York University. Constance Motley remained with the N.A.A.C.P., and she became assistant counsel in 1949 and associate counsel in 1961.

As a lawyer, Constance Motley has been involved in the legal aspects of almost all the important civil rights cases in recent years. She has directed many of the cases, including the court case that resulted in the admission of James Meredith to the University of Mississippi in 1962. In the field of public housing, she has represented many cases that have involved discrimination. In 1963 she traveled approximately 70,000 miles by plane to argue cases in various parts of the country. By early 1964 she argued before the Supreme Court on six occasions, and she won a favorable decision in each of the cases.

In 1964 Constance Motley took on new responsibilities through a vote of confidence by the people of New York. She became the first black woman to be elected to the New York state senate. As state senator, she concentrated on the problems related to fair housing, education, and employment, which were of primary concern in her district.

Because of the respect she had earned and her excellent leadership ability, Constance Motley was elected to another high post. She became president of the borough of Manhattan in New York City in 1965.

In 1966 President Lyndon Johnson selected Constance Motley to be a United States district judge. For her remarkable service, she has received over twenty-five awards and citations from various organizations. Constance Motley lives with her family in New York City where she continues to seek justice for all people.

Finding the Meanings

Match each word in Column A with its meaning in Column B. Write the correct letter of the meaning on the blank before each word in Column A.

Column A	Column B
1. _____ value	a. nearly or about
2. _____ related	b. to pay close attention
3. _____ philanthropist	c. usefulness or importance
4. _____ sincere	d. a discussion of reasons for and against
5. _____ approximately	e. connected in some way
6. _____ debate	f. free from pretense
7. _____ concentrate	g. unusual or worthy of notice
8. _____ remarkable	h. someone who shows goodwill toward humanity by acts of kindness

Understanding the Story

Answer the following questions and statements by using the information given in the story.

1. Where was Constance Motley born? _____

_____

2. Who offered to finance Constance Baker's college education? _____

_____

3. Name two activities Constance Baker Motley took part in during her high school

years. _____

4. What did Joel Motley study during his years in college? _____

_____

5. As state senator, what state did Constance Motley represent? _____

_____

6. Name a very important civil rights case that was directed by Constance Motley.

_____

7. What work did Constance Baker do while she attended law school? _____

_____

8. What well-known person chose Constance Motley to be a United States district

judge? _____

_____

Jesse Owens

TRACK STAR

When the American athletes returned from Germany to their native land after the 1936 Olympics, a new and great champion was among them. His name was Jesse Owens. Crowds greeted the young black athlete as he stepped off the boat at New York City. Thousands cheered as the group of athletes rode at the head of the parade that was held to honor them. Most of all, the crowd cheered for Jesse Owens. This champion had set a new world record in track and had won four gold medals.

The rain during the 1936 Olympics in Berlin, Germany, did not keep the United States from claiming another champion. As a crowd of over one hundred thousand watched, a black youth shot through the finish line like a bolt of lightning. The crowd had been quiet before, but suddenly they were cheering wildly. The people in the stadium, most of them Germans, were proud of this athlete from another country. Jesse Owens had just set a new world record in the 200-meter dash.

Jesse Owens was born on a tenant farm in Alabama and was one of seven children in the Owens family. As a child, he worked in the cotton fields. His mother and father named him James Cleveland Owens, but called him J. C. for short.

When little J. C. went to school and the teacher asked his name, he answered, "J. C. Owens." That was all he knew. His teacher thought that he said Jesse and started calling him by that name. He was a shy little boy and was too bashful to correct the teacher, so Jesse became his name. He never changed it.

In 1924, when Jesse was eleven years old, his parents decided to leave Alabama and move to Cleveland, Ohio. They hoped to find something better for their large family.

Jesse's father went to work in a factory. But the factory soon closed, and Mr. Owens was out of a job. Jesse Owens began looking for work so that he could help his family. He scrubbed floors and did many other odd jobs to make money. Later, the owner of a shoe shop offered young Jesse Owens his first steady job.

The owner was very pleased with Jesse's work. When there were no shoes to be shined, Jesse watched the cobbler mend shoes. Jesse began to hope that he might have his own shoe-repair shop someday.

One day a notice was placed on the bulletin board at Fairmont Junior High where Jesse went to school. It was an invitation for the students to try out for track. Since it was spring, most of the young people jumped at the chance to try out. It meant being out in the fresh air. They would get out of class thirty minutes earlier, too.

The tryouts were held on the sidewalk in front of the school. Chalk was used to mark off the measured distances. Teachers, students, office workers, janitors, and many parents came to watch the try-outs.

The track coach had planned the races well. Students were appointed to time the races with watches. Others kept the sidewalks clean by sweeping them. Still other students kept the crowd back.

Jesse Owens, a small youth compared to those he ran against, won every race he entered. He was the new school champion in track.

Jesse set a record for his junior high school that day. This was his first record. It was also the beginning of a lasting friendship between Jesse Owens and his junior high coach. Jesse began to work hard to improve himself. He loved to win, but he knew how to accept defeat. He ran with such grace that at times it seemed he was not trying hard enough.

Jesse did not always win, however. In 1932 Jesse tried out for the Olympics. He was a junior in high school at that time. Ralph Metcalfe, a great black athlete from Marquette University, defeated Jesse. Metcalfe went on to the Olympics that year and won two Olympic medals.

Although Jesse did not go to the Olympics in 1932, he continued setting new high school records in the 100-yard dash, broad jump, and 220-yard dash. Newspapers across the nation were soon calling him "the greatest one-man track team." Of the many colleges which offered Jesse scholarships, he chose Ohio State University.

While at Ohio State, Jesse Owens became known as the "Buckeye Bullet." To help pay his expenses, Jesse worked at a service station in Columbus. He later worked in the Ohio House of Representatives.

When Jesse tried out for the 1936 Olympics, the competition was great. Ralph Metcalfe and other great stars were there. But Jesse passed the tryouts and was off to Berlin.

At Berlin, he won the 100-meter dash, the broad jump, and the 200-meter dash. He defeated Metcalfe in the 100-meter dash. Four days later he was part of a relay team that won the 400-meter relay. Ralph Metcalfe was also part of this relay team. In the 1936 Olympics Jesse Owens won four gold medals. Few people have ever won as many first-place medals in Olympic competition.

Being a winner meant many things to Jesse Owens. He wanted to win for himself and for his country. Each time he won an event, the American flag was raised above the others. "The Star-Spangled Banner" was also played each time an American won an event. Jesse Owens was proud to bring honor to his race and to his country.

During World War II, the United States government asked Jesse Owens to direct an athletic program for the armed forces. He was happy to do this. He wanted to help train the American soldiers to be physically fit. Jesse Owens felt that he was once again on America's team.

More recently Jesse Owens has continued to work with sports. He has traveled in many countries as an ambassador of goodwill for the United States. Jesse Owens learned that success in life and in sports depends upon fair play, hard work, and good standards. No matter how many medals he has won or how many records he has broken, Jesse Owens has remained an honest and sincere person. He is truly one of America's greatest athletes.

Finding Antonyms

Match each word in Column A with its antonym in Column B. Write the correct letter of the antonym on the blank before each word in Column A.

Column A	Column B
1. _____ quiet	a. large
2. _____ proud	b. many
3. _____ fresh	c. loud
4. _____ small	d. changing
5. _____ beginning	e. stale
6. _____ success	f. modest
7. _____ steady	g. ending
8. _____ few	h. failure

Reviewing the Story

Fill in each blank with the word or group of words which completes each sentence correctly.

1. As the crowd cheered, Jesse Owens set a new world record in the _____ _____.

2. Jesse was named _____ by his parents and was called _____ for short.

3. In 1932 Jesse tried out for the Olympics but was defeated by _____ _____.

4. The 1936 Olympics were held in _____ .

5. While Jesse was competing in track at Ohio State University, he was nicknamed

   the " _____ ."

6. Jesse has often helped the United States by traveling to other countries as an

   _____ .

Understanding the Story

Answer the following questions by using the information given in the story.

1. How many gold medals did Jesse Owens win in the 1936 Olympics? _____

   _____

2. When Jesse began his first steady job, what kind of work did he do? _____

   _____

3. When did Jesse set his very first track record? _____

   _____

4. What did the United States government ask Jesse Owens to do during World

   War II? _____

   _____

5. Why has Jesse Owens been so successful in life? _____

   _____

Leontyne Price

SINGER

Leontyne Price made music history when she sang at the opening of the new Metropolitan Opera House in New York's Lincoln Center. She was chosen to sing the leading role in a new opera, *Antony and Cleopatra.* Famous singers everywhere envied her. But they all agreed that she was "the queen of the operatic world."

The "girl with the golden voice" was born in Laurel, Mississippi. When Leontyne was two years old, a local music teacher sensed that the child might have a talent for music. When Mrs. Price heard this, she answered, "Well, I have prayed for it. If Leontyne wants music, she'll get it."

A few years later, Mrs. Price kept her promise. When Leontyne was four-and-a-half years old, she got her first piano lesson. Her parents did not have the money to buy a real piano, so Leontyne had to practice on a toy piano. Mr. Price was a carpenter, and his wife worked as a midwife. When they could not afford the two-dollar lesson fee, Leontyne's mother would do the teacher's washing and ironing to help pay for the lesson.

How happy Leontyne was when she no longer had to practice on that toy piano! Her parents bought her a real one. As a down payment Mr. and Mrs. Price traded their Victrola. Mr. Price hesitated because the Victrola was one of their nicest possessions. But since he wanted to please his family, he agreed to buy the piano.

At first Mr. Price had very little interest in the music lessons. But when Leontyne played in a piano recital, he changed his mind. He was very proud of his young daughter. He seemed to be even prouder than his wife.

As Leontyne Price became older, she began to think of what she wanted her career in life to be. At one time she thought about teaching. She prepared herself for teaching by earning a degree from Central State College in Wilberforce, Ohio. While in school, however, Leontyne continued to study music. During her last year in college, her teachers felt that she should sing for the public rather than teach. They urged her to apply for a scholarship in music. Leontyne Price won the scholarship.

Leontyne's parents were both happy and sad when they heard about the scholarship. They were happy that Leontyne had been blessed with such a beautiful voice. And they were happy that she had received such an honor. But how could she accept this honor? The thought of having to refuse the offer made them very sad. They just did not have enough money to help finance a music career.

But, as so often happens in life, the Price family had friends who wanted to help. The Alexander Chisholm family became a second family for Leontyne Price. Mr. Chisholm, a banker, and his wife had become interested in Leontyne Price a few years earlier, when Leontyne's aunt had taken a job in the banker's home. They had helped provide money for her while she was in Central State College. When she received the scholarship, they again wanted to help.

Today when Leontyne Price talks about her family, she always includes Mrs. Chisholm. She calls her a second mother. The color of Leontyne's skin did not matter to Mrs. Chisholm. She saw Leontyne Price as a lovely young girl with a beautiful voice. She wanted to help her get the best training possible.

Leontyne Price has always been serious about her work. Shortly after she entered the Juilliard School of Music in New York City, she became interested in opera. She began to appear in student productions. Ira Gershwin heard her and gave her the leading role in an opera, *Porgy and Bess*. Her singing partner was the famous baritone, William Warfield. They later married. Singing in this opera gave Leontyne Price the chance to be heard.

Numerous people did hear her, and they liked what they heard. Music critics praised her singing and her excellent acting. Many composers asked Leontyne Price to introduce their new works.

By 1955 people everywhere had heard about Leontyne Price, the new black star of opera. Leontyne Price says that after appearing in *Porgy and Bess* she was more determined than ever to succeed in opera. She loved every minute of it. Then she was given the title role in the opera *Tosca*. With this opera she became the first black person to appear in an opera on television.

In 1959 Leontyne Price became a grand opera star in another country. She went to Vienna to star in the opera *Aïda*. She was a great success. This led to her being invited to star at the Metropolitan Opera in New York. When she finished singing the leading role of Leonora in Verdi's *Il Trovatore* at the Metropolitan, the audience gave her the longest ovation in the history of the opera company. It lasted forty-two minutes.

Leontyne Price has been successful offstage, too. She has received many awards. In 1964 she was one of thirty Americans selected to receive the Freedom Medal. This is the highest American civil honor. President Johnson presented the award and said, "Her singing has brought light to her land." During the same year, Leontyne Price was the only American to accompany the La Scala Opera Company of Italy on its visit to Russia. In 1965 she received the Italian Award of Merit for her contribution to Italian music.

Leontyne Price has often been asked what her secret of success has been. There are many fine singers, but very few are able to become great opera stars. First of all, Leontyne says that she loves to sing. "You must like what you are doing if you want to be happy and successful." She can't remember when she didn't have a desire to be on the stage. "This is why I became the 'opera bug' that I am."

And she laughs when she admits that she is a "born show-off."

Success and fame have not spoiled Leontyne Price. She has not forgotten those who were there to help her as she began her career. Her mother says, "Leontyne never changes. Laurel, Mississippi, loves her. When she comes for a visit, she is still the same Leontyne." As a child Leontyne sang in her church choir. Today, when she is at home, she always attends church and sings one or two songs. She visits her old school and talks with the teachers and children. She is an inspiration for the students. She is never too busy to see them when they come to her home.

Although Leontyne Price has been successful, she says, "I still have to work hard at my career. But I would like to give of my time and myself to help others. I want to help young people." To do this, she has engaged in civic work. She has helped the Dorothy Maynor School of Arts project. This project provides lessons for children in Harlem at prices they can afford. She also helps to raise money for the United Negro College Fund.

Leontyne Price has reached the top of the world of opera. She has been honored both at home and abroad. She has been called "the voice of the century." Hard work has brought her success. This success makes her happy, but it makes her even happier to have gained it also for those whom she calls "my people."

Understanding the Story

Answer the following questions and statements by using the information given in the story.

1. Name three operas in which Leontyne Price has performed in the leading roles.

----

2. How did the Alexander Chrisholm family help Leontyne? ----------------

----

----

3. How do we know that fame and success have not changed Leontyne Price's

personality? --

----

4. Name two awards Leontyne Price has received. _____

_____

_____

5. List some of the ways Mr. and Mrs. Price helped their daughter to develop her

musical talents. _____

_____

_____

Reviewing the Story

Fill in each blank with the correct word or group of words. Each answer will be used only once.

Freedom Medal	United Negro College Fund	toy
Ira Gershwin	scholarship	piano
Chisholm	William Warfield	

1. Leontyne was four-and-a-half when she received her first _____ lesson.

2. For a while, Leontyne Price practiced on a _____ piano.

3. Leontyne applied for and won a _____ in music.

4. The _____ family was like a second family to Leontyne.

5. When _____ heard Leontyne Price sing, he gave her the leading role in *Porgy and Bess*.

6. _____ was Leontyne's singing partner in *Porgy and Bess*.

7. In 1964 Leontyne Price received the _____.

8. Leontyne Price is engaged in civic work, and she helps young people by raising money for the _____.

Finding Synonyms

Match each word in Column A with its synonym in Column B. Write the correct letter of the synonym on the blank before each word in Column A.

Column A

1. _____ talent

2. _____ promise

3. _____ carpenter

4. _____ career

5. _____ recital

6. _____ prepare

7. _____ ovation

8. _____ award

Column B

a. concert

b. woodworker

c. prize

d. ability

e. applause

f. business

g. pledge

h. arrange

Wilma G. Rudolph

ATHLETE

There was great excitement in Wilma Rudolph's hometown when the news of her great achievement was announced. She had won three gold medals at the 1960 Olympic Games in Rome, Italy. For her excellence she had been named "Female Athlete of the Year" for 1960. Those who knew her well were overjoyed. Wilma Rudolph, the girl who had once been a cripple, had become a great track star.

Wilma Glodean Rudolph was born in 1940 in a tiny community in Tennessee. She weighed about four pounds at birth, and there was little hope that she would live. But Wilma's family gave her a lot of love and care, and she slowly began to gain strength.

Four years later Wilma was ill again. This time she had two very serious diseases, scarlet fever and pneumonia. Either disease could have been fatal, but Wilma began to get better. However, the sickness affected one of Wilma's legs. She was unable to walk.

Wilma was young to have such a fight ahead of her. But she wanted to walk, and she became a brave little fighter. She was helped because her mother was a fighter, too. Mrs. Rudolph believed that her daughter would walk again and was determined to help her. The next few years after Wilma's illness were very hard ones for the Rudolph family, but they did what was necessary to help Wilma.

For two years Wilma had to have special medical treatments. Once a week Mrs. Rudolph would bundle her small child in a blanket and go by bus to a hospital in Nashville, Tennessee. This was about a two-hour ride from their home in Clarksville. In time Wilma began to improve, but she had to wear special shoes.

Wilma became interested in sports when she was eleven years old. She tried not to let her weak leg keep her from doing anything that she wanted to do. She tried no matter how hard it was or how clumsy she might be.

Since Wilma and her brothers were interested in basketball, they set up a basketball hoop in the yard so that they could play at home. Wilma began to play with her brothers every day. The game was fun for her, and it was good for her legs.

With hard work on her part, Wilma continued to improve. She just would not give up. When she entered high school, she became a part of the girls' basketball team. Her coach, C. C. Gray, taught her how to play the game well. He said she was just like a little mosquito—always buzzing around. By the time she was fifteen, she had become an excellent basketball player. She even set a new record for her high school. Wilma seemed to be making up for all the time she had lost when she was so sick.

While at the 1955 State Basketball Tournament in Nashville, Wilma Rudolph was introduced to track. Mr. Edward Temple, the women's track coach at Tennessee A. & I. State University, felt that Wilma would make a good sprinter. He asked her high school coach to form a girls' track team.

Wilma Rudolph soon found that she enjoyed running track more than playing basketball. In three years of high school competition, she never lost a race. Wilma liked to run, and she worked very hard at learning how to run faster. During the summer months, she and her high school coach drove to Nashville every day to work with Mr. Temple.

In 1957 Wilma Rudolph entered Tennessee A. and I. State University. She soon became one of the school's greatest stars. She was also a very busy student. She worked four hours each day in a campus office. She ran at least two hours a day. Her coach held three track workouts every day. Despite this schedule, Wilma was able to keep a "B" average in her studies.

America was proud of Wilma Rudolph at the 1960 Olympics in Rome, Italy. She defeated those running against her and set three Olympic records. Her team set a world record for the 400-meter relay.

Since the 1960 Olympics, Wilma Rudolph has received many honors and awards. She realizes that in sports not only the winning is important. Therefore she is very proud of the trophy that she received in 1961 for advancing sportsmanship.

Wilma Rudolph has continued her interest in track by helping many other young women who also love to run. She is a winning person as well as a winning athlete. For this reason the United States government has sent her to many countries of the world as an ambassador of goodwill.

Wilma Rudolph is considered a model for many young athletes. Her first steps in life were slow. But many races are won in the home stretch. She overcame her handicap by constant exercise. The work was hard and painful at times, but Wilma Rudolph set her goal and worked toward that end. She won her race. She became a champion.

Reviewing the Story

Fill in each blank with the word or group of words which completes each sentence correctly.

1. Wilma Rudolph won _____ gold medals in the 1960 Olympic Games.

2. As a child, a serious illness affected one of Wilma's _____, and she could not _____.

3. The game of _____ helped to strengthen her weak leg.

4. Wilma began to enjoy running _____ more than playing _____.

5. Wilma has been sent to many countries by the United States government as an _____.

6. In 1961 Wilma received a _____ for her work in advancing _____.

Finding Homonyms

The words listed below appear in the story. Write a homonym for each of the words.

1. sent _____

2. two _____

3. knew _____

4. by _____

5. would _____

6. weak _____

7. there _____

8. great _____

Understanding the Story

Answer the following questions by using the information given in the story.

1. Besides winning three gold medals, what other special honor did Wilma receive in 1960? _____

_____

2. How did Wilma's mother help her when she was very ill? _____

_____

_____

_____

3. Where were the 1960 Olympic Games held? _____

_____

4. Why is Wilma Rudolph a model for many young athletes? _____

_____

_____

5. What two serious diseases did Wilma Rulodph have as a child, and how did the

illnesses affect her body? _____

_____

_____

Jeanne Spurlock

PSYCHIATRIST

Jeanne Spurlock developed an interest in medicine while she was quite young. She saw the pain and poverty which many people faced and decided that she would devote a great part of her life toward helping to relieve suffering. Therefore, after graduating from high school and college, she attended Howard University College of Medicine. After receiving a Doctor of Medicine degree in 1947, she entered the internship program at Provident Hospital in Chicago to become a psychiatrist. When the internship was concluded, she entered a two-year residency program in psychiatry at Cook County Psychopathic Hospital in Chicago.

In 1950 Dr. Spurlock received a fellowship award in child psychiatry from the Institute for Juvenile Research in Chicago. After completing this special training, she became a staff psychiatrist for the Institute and for a mental health clinic, as well as a consultant for the Illinois School for the Deaf.

In 1953 Dr. Spurlock began a seven-year appointment in adult and child psychoanalytic training at the Chicago Institute for Psychoanalysis. During that time, she also served as assistant professor of psychiatry at the University of Illinois College of Medicine. From 1960 to 1968 Dr. Spurlock served as attending psychiatrist at Michael Reese Hospital in Chicago and became clinical assistant professor of psychiatry at the University of Illinois College of Medicine.

Dr. Spurlock had a private practice in psychiatry from 1951 to 1968 and practiced her skills in psychoanalysis from 1960 to 1968. In 1968 she became chairperson of the department of psychiatry at Meharry Medical College in Nashville, Tennessee. While holding this position until 1973, Dr. Spurlock was a member of major committees in her field and maintained other teaching positions. She then spent a year working for the National Institute of Mental Health. In 1974 she became deputy medical director for the American Psychiatric Association located in Washington, D.C. She also joined the staffs of Howard University College of Medicine and George Washington University College of Medicine as clinical professor of psychiatry.

Dr. Jeanne Spurlock has published articles in several professional journals and is a member of many professional organizations in general medicine and in psychiatry. She has also received many honors and awards. In 1971 she was the recipient of the Strecker Award, pre- sented annually by the Institute of the Pennsylvania Hospital, for her outstanding contributions to psychiatric care and treatment. She was the first woman and the first black American to receive this award. In 1974 Dr. Spurlock received the Professional Leadership Award from the Section on Psychiatry and Neurology of the National Medical Association.

Understanding the Story

Answer the following questions and statements by using the information given in the story.

1. Why did Dr. Spurlock wish to enter the medical profession? _____

_____

_____

2. From what school did Dr. Spurlock receive a Doctor of Medicine degree? _____

_____

3. At what hospital did Dr. Spurlock complete a two-year residency in psychiatry?

_____

_____

4. What position did Dr. Spurlock hold at Michael Reese Hospital? _____

_____

5. Name two of the many awards that Dr. Jeanne Spurlock has received for her out-

standing work. _____

_____

6. What position does Dr. Spurlock hold with the American Psychiatric Association?

_____

7. Where is Meharry Medical College located? _____

_____

8. What position did Dr. Spurlock hold on the faculty of Meharry Medical College?

----

9. Name some of the positions Dr. Spurlock has held since 1968. --------------------

----

Finding the Meanings

Match each word in Column A with its meaning in Column B. Write the correct letter of the meaning on the blank before each word in Column A.

Column A

Column B

1. --------- devote

a. position held by a doctor who practices in a hospital after completing an internship

2. --------- internship

b. a person who gives professional advice

3. --------- residency

c. a teacher of the highest rank in a university or college

4. --------- psychiatry

d. to give a certain time completely to some activity

5. --------- consultant

e. a person who receives something

6. --------- psychoanalysis

f. position or service as an apprentice

7. --------- professor

g. the minute examination of a mind or personality

8. --------- recipient

h. the study and treatment of mental disorders

Harriet Tubman

CHAMPION OF FREEDOM

On a bronze tablet in front of the courthouse in Auburn, New York, there is a statement about a brave woman "whose charity was unbounded, whose wisdom, integrity, and patriotism enabled her to perform wonders in the cause of freedom." This woman, Harriet Tubman, was born about forty years before the Civil War. She lived on a plantation in Maryland with her parents and eleven brothers and sisters.

As a child, Harriet was very stubborn and strong willed. She had the dark skin and the fighting spirit of her African ancestors, the Ashanti people. Before she was ten years old, Harriet began to rebel against her way of life and the conditions around her.

Harriet Tubman spent the first twenty-six years of her life as a slave. After she married John Tubman, a free black, she too wanted to be free. She decided to run away from the master of her plantation. She thought she could find her freedom in the North.

Running away was a very dangerous thing for a slave to do. But Harriet Tub-man was not afraid. Only one of two things could happen. She could reach the North and be free, or she could die trying.

Harriet Tubman did not want to go alone. She asked her husband to go with her, but he refused. Finally two of her brothers agreed to go with her. After they started on their long journey, the brothers became afraid. Before dawn, they returned to their slave house and made Harriet come back with them.

Thoughts of not being free continued to bother Harriet Tubman. The next week she again started out. This time she was alone and without money. She had nothing but a determined mind and nerves of steel. Having never learned to read and write, she could not use the road signs to guide her. She knew that she had to go north, so she used the North Star as her guide. During the trip she faced many dangers. The greatest danger, of course, was being captured.

The long journey to freedom was rough. Harriet Tubman traveled at night and slept in hiding during the day. She waded upstream through rivers to escape bloodhounds trained to trail runaway slaves. Friendly Quakers along the way gave her food and shelter. Many white people and free blacks gave her directions along the way. She was almost caught many times by slave patrols that rode the highways looking for runaway slaves. After many days on the road, Harriet Tubman finally reached the free soil of Pennsylvania.

When Harriet Tubman reached Philadelphia, she went to work and saved all the money she could. Then she moved on to other northern cities so that slave hunters could not trace her.

Harriet Tubman's first thoughts as a free woman were of her people. "They should be free, too. I must help others escape," she said. Harriet Tubman began to make plans for returning to the slave territory. She could not be happy as long as her family and others were enslaved. She knew that she might be caught, but she was willing to take the chance. She decided to dedicate her life toward helping others.

In order to help other slaves, Harriet Tubman knew that she had to learn all she could about the Underground Railroad. This was not a real railroad. It was a group of people who helped runaway slaves on their way to the North. The people hid and fed the slaves and helped them find the next friendly family or "station." Harriet Tubman needed to know where these "stations" were.

At last the day came for her to return to the slave territory. She had learned most of the tricks about the Underground Railroad. Her friends had told her about the slave traps. She was now ready to go south. Harriet Tubman started the work that would make her famous as a liberator of slaves.

Helping other slaves to escape was dangerous business, but fear did not stop Harriet Tubman. She returned south nineteen times. Slaveholders began to lose so many slaves that a large reward was offered for her capture. In ten years she led more than three hundred slaves to freedom. She was never caught, and she never lost a "passenger" on her "railroad."

Once on the road, Harriet Tubman ruled the slaves with a firm hand. Until they were free, she was their new master. Some slaves became frightened along the way. They also were cold, tired, and hungry. Some of them began to think that the plantation wasn't so bad after all. But when slaves wanted to turn back, Harriet Tubman drove them on. If the slaves returned to the plantation, they might give away the escape plans. The plans had to be kept secret. To control the slaves, Harriet Tubman kept a pistol in the folds of her dress. Many times she would point the gun at a frightened slave and say, "You will go, or you'll die here." They always moved on.

When the law was passed that allowed slave catchers to seize and return slaves to the South, Harriet Tubman began to take slaves to Canada, where slave catchers were not allowed. The runaway slaves were taken from Maryland to Canada by train. Many friends, white and black, gave her money for train fare, food, and clothing. Harriet Tubman did not rest until her wards were on free soil.

When the question of slavery divided our country, Harriet Tubman volunteered in the Union Army. She served as a nurse, scout, and spy. One official record states that "she became the only woman in American history to plan an expedition against armed forces."

Harriet Tubman organized freed slaves to serve as scouts and spies. They moved quietly through battle lines without being seen. Because of her leadership ability, she was often called "General Tubman."

After the Civil War, Harriet Tubman bought a small farm near Auburn, New York. Although she was not as active as she had been in the past, she spent the rest of her life helping others in every way that she could.

Harriet Tubman was almost one hundred years old when she died. Shortly before her death, the Queen of England sent her a Diamond Jubilee Medal. Other nations of the world joined England in honoring Harriet Tubman. They recognized that she had lived and worked for freedom.

Reviewing the Story

Underline the word or group of words which completes each sentence correctly.

1. As a child, Harriet Tubman lived on a plantation in **(a) Alabama** **(b) Maryland** **(c) Kentucky** with her family.

2. While journeying to freedom, Harriet traveled during the **(a) morning** **(b) afternoon** **(c) night** .

3. During her journey, Harriet Tubman worked and saved her money when she reached **(a) Philadelphia** **(b) Pittsburgh** **(c) Cleveland** .

4. Harriet returned south **(a) fifteen** **(b) sixteen** **(c) nineteen** times to help other slaves escape.

5. Harriet Tubman was a slave for the first **(a) twenty** **(b) sixteen** **(c) twenty-six** years of her life.

6. When runaway slaves wanted to turn back, Harriet **(a) would** **(b) would not** let them.

7. Harriet Tubman was often called **(a) Captain Harriet** **(b) General Tubman** **(c) Captain Tubman** because of her leadership ability.

8. Harriet Tubman received a Diamond Jubilee Medal from the **(a) King of England** **(b) Queen of France** **(c) Queen of England** .

9. When Harriet Tubman traveled to freedom, she used the **(a) sun** **(b) North Star** **(c) moon** as her guide.

10. During the Civil War, Harriet Tubman served in the Union Army as a spy, scout, and **(a) musician** **(b) doctor** **(c) nurse** .

11. Harriet Tubman died near the age of **(a) one hundred** **(b) sixty** **(c) fifty** .

Finding the Meanings

With the help of a dictionary, write a short meaning for each of the following words.

1. integrity _____

2. ancestors _____

3. refuse _____

4. dawn _____

5. dedicate _____

6. liberator _____

7. volunteer _____

8. patrol _____

Arthur R. Ashe, Jr.

ATHLETE, SOCIAL ACTIVIST, AND WRITER

Arthur Ashe grew up near the only tennis courts in Richmond, Virginia, that were open to blacks. As a child Arthur spent hour after hour on the court practicing with a borrowed racket. Arthur's father just shook his head. As far as he could tell, tennis would always be a game for whites only.

Ashe was born in 1943 in Richmond. His mother, who died when he was only six, taught him to read when he was four years old. His father raised Arthur and his brother to be polite and helpful and to look on the bright side.

Arthur received his first tennis lessons from a young player named Ron Charity. Ron could see that Arthur had a talent for tennis. He gave Arthur's name to a man named Dr. Johnson in Lynchburg. Every summer Dr. Johnson coached young black players at his home. When he was ten, Arthur began spending the summers with Dr. Johnson.

Dr. Johnson taught his young players more than tennis. He taught them good manners. Tennis was still an almost all-white game. Many tennis clubs would not even allow blacks to use their courts or to enter their tournaments. Dr. Johnson knew that some whites would look for any excuse to keep blacks out of the game. So Dr. Johnson taught his players to play balls that were a few inches over the line as though they were good. He cautioned them never to lose their tempers.

When Arthur was 11, he was turned away from a Richmond city tennis tournament because he was black. This was just one of many contests he was not allowed to enter.

At the age of 17, Arthur won the American Tennis Association junior indoor singles title. He won it again the next year. Richard Hudlin, a retired tennis official, offered to coach Ashe. During his senior year in high school, Arthur lived with Hudlin in St. Louis, Missouri.

When Arthur graduated from high school, he accepted a tennis scholarship from the University of California at Los Angeles. In 1963 Arthur became the first black person to play on the U.S. Junior Davis Cup team. He won his Davis Cup match against Venezuela. Ashe would continue to be a part of the U.S. Davis Cup for the next ten years.

In 1964 Ashe's amateur ranking was third, but he had never won a major title. Some tennis players thought Arthur didn't have the will to win. After all, he never showed any emotion on the court. They thought that he just did not care whether he won. These players did not realize that Arthur was just behaving as his father and Dr. Johnson had taught him.

As a senior in college, Arthur won the National Collegiate Athletic Association singles and doubles titles. Ashe graduated from UCLA with a degree in business administration. Then he enlisted in the army. The army gave Arthur a desk job and allowed him to continue playing tennis.

Ashe's breakthrough year was 1968. At Wimbledon he won his first set but lost the game. Then he won the U.S. Amateur championship. Finally, Arthur won his first major singles tournament, the United States Open Tennis Championships at Forest Hills. His ranking moved to number one!

Ashe was the first black man to win at Forest Hills. He had helped to integrate tennis in the U.S. But there was still one place Arthur Ashe wanted to play— South Africa. He applied many times, but the answer was always the same. South Africa did not allow blacks to compete against whites. The South African government would not even let Ashe visit the country because he was against apartheid, the separation of whites and blacks. At last in 1973, Arthur played in the South African Open. Arthur never forgot the people he met in South Africa. He tried to help them win their rights by protesting U.S. policies toward South Africa.

Arthur was not only concerned with the rights of black people. He also felt that tennis players should have a greater voice in how their sport was run. In 1974 he helped found the Association of Men's Tennis Professionals. Ashe served as its president for five years.

In 1975 Ashe found himself back on the courts of Wimbledon. In the final match, Ashe faced Jimmy Connors. Most people thought Connors was a sure bet to win. They were wrong. Arthur Ashe beat Connors three sets to one.

Arthur Ashe's professional tennis career ended in 1979. In that year he had a mild heart attack. Although Arthur could no longer play tennis, he coached the U.S. Davis Cup team. He worked with the American Heart Association and the United Negro College Fund. He also set up the Safe Passage Foundation to help young black tennis players.

Arthur loved to read about the history of blacks in sports, but there was little on the subject. Arthur spent years doing research on blacks in many different sports. His history, A Hard Road to Glory, was published in 1988. Ashe also wrote a regular newspaper column and two books about his life, Arthur Ashe, Portrait in Motion and Days of Grace: A Memoir.

In 1983 Ashe had a heart bypass operation. In the hospital he was given a blood transfusion. The blood had not been tested for HIV, the virus that causes AIDS. In 1988 Arthur learned that he had gotten AIDS from the transfusion. Instead of slowing down, Arthur worked harder than ever. He set up the Arthur Ashe Foundation for the Defeat of AIDS. He spent time with his wife and young daughter and continued to work for many good causes.

Arthur Ashe died in 1993. People throughout the U.S. were saddened by his loss. Arthur Ashe was more than a great tennis player. He was a patient, intelligent, caring man who showed how much difference one person can make.

Finding Synonyms

Match each word in Column A with its synonym in Column B. Write the correct letter of the synonym on the blank before each word in Column A.

Column A	Column B
1. _____ talent	a. warn
2. _____ coach	b. last
3. _____ caution	c. take
4. _____ tournament	d. join
5. _____ accept	e. instruct
6. _____ major	f. contest
7. _____ emotion	g. smart
8. _____ enlist	h. feeling
9. _____ final	i. ability
10. _____ intelligent	j. important

Understanding the Story

Write true or false before each of the following statements.

1. _____ Arthur Ashe grew up near a tennis court.

2. _____ Arthur's father taught Arthur how to play tennis.

3. _____ Arthur Ashe was never turned away from a tennis tournament because of his race.

4. _____ The University of California offered Arthur a tennis scholarship.

5. _____ Many players believed that Arthur showed too much emotion during tennis games.

6. _____ Arthur Ashe defeated Jimmy Connors to win Wimbledon in 1975.

7. _____ Ashe's book *A Hard Road to Glory* is about black soldiers.

Daniel Hale Williams

SURGEON

One morning in 1893 the words "Sewed Up the Human Heart" headlined a Chicago newspaper. People everywhere read the story with great excitement. Earlier that day a young black doctor had actually sewed up a cut in a person's heart. This operation had never been done before. But before the day was over, the name of this young doctor, Daniel Hale Williams, was being discussed everywhere. He was the first doctor to operate successfully on the human heart. And his patient lived!

One night Dr. Williams was on duty when a man was brought into Chicago's Provident Hospital. The man had been stabbed with a knife. The knife had cut into the man's heart, and the man was bleeding very badly. Being the daring young doctor that he was, Dr. Williams was willing to try almost anything to save the man's life. He didn't have much to work with except his great medical skill.

In 1893 many of the modern medical tools of today were unknown. Dr. Williams did not have the use of an "artificial heart." The use of X-ray photographs,

modern miracle drugs, and blood transfusions was uncommon at that time. But with the help of six other doctors, Dr. Williams sewed up the wound in the man's heart as it continued to beat. This heart operation became one of the most famous operations in medical history.

Even as a child Daniel Williams had a strong drive and desire to succeed in the things that he did. Daniel was born in Pennsylvania in 1858. He was from a large family of one brother and five sisters.

Daniel attended school and was a good student. He loved to read, and his parents bought him many books. After his father's death, Daniel's mother decided to take her children and move to Wisconsin. She left Daniel behind with friends so that he could finish the school year.

The people who kept Daniel were good to him, but he was not happy. He felt deserted. He missed his mother and his brother and sisters. When he could stand being away from his family no longer, he decided to run away. He hated to leave his books, but they were too heavy to carry. He took the few clothes that he had and left the home of his friends. He had no money, but he could think only of finding his family.

When Daniel reached the railroad station, he told the ticket agent that he had no money but that he wanted to see his mother. The agent felt sorry for Daniel and allowed him to ride free.

When Mrs. Williams saw Daniel, she was too happy to see him to scold him for running away. Within a few days Daniel enrolled in school. Mrs. Williams could not afford to buy him new books, so he entered school with a dictionary as his only book.

Daniel soon knew many words. He used his dictionary to find the meanings of new words—words that he had heard or was just curious about. He loved to read and was especially interested in science and history.

Daniel learned early in life that everyone has to work for the things desired. At the age of twelve he began to work and earn his own living. He worked in the barber shop of a family friend. His mother helped him pay his way through elementary school and an academy in Wisconsin. But she did not have the money to send him to college.

After completing his work at the academy, Daniel thought of becoming a lawyer. But studying law did not satisfy Daniel Williams, so he soon gave up the idea of becoming a lawyer. He decided that he wanted to be a doctor.

Williams got a lucky chance to study medicine in the office of a famous army doctor who had worked with President U. S. Grant. Daniel Williams worked for the doctor and studied his medical books after doing the office chores. The older doctor in the office taught him about medicine. After two years, Daniel Williams passed a test and entered medical school in Chicago. To help pay his expenses, this young medical student played in an orchestra on a sight-seeing boat that toured Lake Michigan.

When Dr. Williams graduated from Northwestern University Medical School, he remained there as a teacher. At that time large universities rarely employed black teachers. But Williams had been a good student, and the university felt he would be a good teacher.

After teaching for one year, Dr. Williams began his practice of medicine in Chicago. In a very short time he had become a member of the Illinois State Board of Health. Along with maintaining a busy practice, Dr. Williams tried to help many young blacks in Chicago who wanted to become doctors. In those days Chicago hospitals did not accept blacks as beginning doctors. There were no training schools for black women who wanted to enter the medical profession. In order to provide training for qualified medical students, regardless of their color, Dr. Williams began raising money to build Provident Hospital in Chicago.

Through the hard work of many doctors and the cooperation of the city of Chicago and state of Illinois, in 1891 Provident Hospital was opened. Connected with it was the first training school for black nurses in the United States.

After Provident Hospital was opened, Dr. Williams helped to organize other hospitals for men and women of the black race.

Dr. Daniel Hale Williams lived to be seventy-three years old. He is remembered not only as a great doctor but also as a person who helped other doctors and students who shared his aim of serving humanity through medical science.

Finding Homonyms

Match each word in Column A with its homonym in Column B. Write the correct letter of the homonym on the blank before each word in Column A.

Column A

1. _____ one
2. _____ read
3. _____ great
4. _____ sew
5. _____ to
6. _____ no
7. _____ see
8. _____ for
9. _____ new
10. _____ be
11. _____ their
12. _____ would

Column B

a. too
b. bee
c. won
d. fore
e. wood
f. so
g. knew
h. grate
i. sea
j. red
k. there
l. know

Reviewing the Story

Underline the word or group of words which completes each sentence correctly.

1. Dr. Williams performed the first successful operation on the human   **(a) lungs** **(b) heart** **(c) kidneys** .

2. In **(a) 1893** **(b) 1873** **(c) 1895** headlines about the skillful operation performed by Dr. Williams appeared in the newspapers.

3. Daniel ran away to join his family in   **(a) Illinois** **(b) Michigan** **(c) Wisconsin** .

4. When Daniel found his family and entered school, the only book he had was a **(a) reader** **(b) dictionary** .

5. Daniel worked at his first job at the age of **(a) eight** **(b) fifteen** **(c) twelve** .

6. Before studying medicine, Daniel Hale Williams had thought of becoming a

    (a) lawyer **(b) farmer** **(c) dentist** .

7. To help pay his expenses in medical school, Daniel Williams **(a) worked on a farm**

    (b) taught musical lesson **(c) played in an orchestra** .

8. Dr. Williams began practicing medicine in **(a) New York City** **(b) Chicago**

    (c) Detroit .

9. The hospital in Chicago that Dr. Williams raised money to build was named

    (a) Provident **(b) Bellevue** **(c) Massachusetts General** .

10. Dr. Williams died at the age of **(a) eighty** **(b) seventy-six** **(c) seventy-three** .

11. Dr. Daniel Hale Williams was born in **(a) Ohio** **(b) Michigan** **(c) Pennsylvania**

    in 1858.

12. When Daniel Williams was a child, he especially enjoyed reading books about

    history and **(a) music** **(b) science** **(c) farming** .

ANSWERS TO THE EXERCISES

PAGE 9
Understanding the Story—1. d; 2. i; 3. f; 4. c; 5. a; 6. g; 7. j; 8. e; 9. h; 10. b; 11. l; 12. k

PAGE 10
Finding Synonyms—1. find; 2. better; 3. unfolded; 4. complete; 5. shun; 6. lucky; 7. helpful; 8. liability; 9. area; 10. purchase

PAGES 13 AND 14
Reviewing the Story—1. New Orleans; 2. mouth; 3. tambourine; 4. bugle; 5. cornet; 6. Waif's Home for Boys; 7. played with a band; 8. fifty cents; 9. Ambassador of Jazz; 10. imitate

PAGE 14
Finding Antonyms—1. artificial; 2. drab; 3. smooth; 4. earlier; 5. failure; 6. inactive; 7. follower; 8. catch

PAGE 17
Finding the Meanings—1. d; 2. f; 3. e; 4. g; 5. a; 6. h; 7. b; 8. c

PAGES 17 AND 18
Understanding the Story—1. true; 2. false; 3. true; 4. false; 5. true; 6. false

PAGE 18
Reviewing the Story—1. b; 2. a; 3. c; 4. a; 5. c; 6. b

PAGES 20 AND 21
Reviewing the Story—1. slaves, free; 2. rice, cotton; 3. five miles; 4. dressmaker; 5. missionary; 6. six; 7. Franklin Roosevelt; 8. Cookman Institute

PAGE 21
Finding Synonyms—1. f; 2. e; 3. b; 4. h; 5. d; 6. a; 7. c; 8. g

PAGES 23 AND 24
Understanding the Story—1. Jamaica; 2. leader; 3. Georgia, training; 4. Vietnam, enemy; 5. stick; 6. helicopter; 7. Reagan; 8. Chairman of the Joint Chiefs of Staff

Finding Synonyms—1. f; 2. e; 3. b; 4. h; 5. d; 6. a; 7. c; 8. g

PAGES 26 AND 27
Understanding the Story—1. Gwendolyn Brooks was thirteen years old. 2. She was chosen as one of "Ten Women of the Year." 3. Her greatest literary award was the Pulitzer Prize. 4. Her first book of poems was published in 1945. 5. A writer must be able to see and understand people in their daily lives. A writer must be able to see beauty where it does not exist and be able to describe it for others to see and enjoy. 6. Her work can be understood by everyone because she writes about the things that people think, see, and feel. 7. Gwendolyn's mother played and wrote music. Her father worked in a music publishing house. Gwendolyn's brother was an artist.

PAGE 27
Finding the Meanings—1. d; 2. f; 3. a; 4. h; 5. c; 6. g; 7. e; 8. b

PAGE 30
Finding the Meanings—1. independent; 2. associate; 3. difficult; 4. confidence; 5. supervise; 6. potential; 7. vacant; 8. return
Understanding the Story—1. d; 2. f; 3. a; 4. g; 5. b; 6. h; 7. c; 8. e

PAGE 33
Reviewing the Story—1. great pianist; 2. Rogues of Rhythm; 3. King Cole; 4. his family, music, baseball; 5. Los Angeles Little League team
Finding Synonyms—1. support; 2. planned; 3. easy; 4. truthful; 5. like; 6. endless; 7. ability; 8. opposed; 9. performer; 10. threesome

PAGE 34
Understanding the Story—1. Mrs. Coles helped Nat with his homework, gave Nat music lessons, and helped his piano practice by playing the piano with him. 2. Nat Cole's father was a Baptist minister. 3. The King Cole Trio reached the top of the list of jazz groups. 4. Nat King Cole was a jazz pianist, a singer, a radio and television star, a movie star, and the head of his own business firm. 5. Nat Cole began appearing in musical shows so he could entertain children as well as adults.

PAGE 37
Finding Antonyms—*Antonyms will vary. Suggested:* 1. discourage; 2. bottom; 3. discontinue; 4. seldom; 5. forget; 6. disrespect; 7. foolish; 8. lighthearted

PAGES 37 AND 38
Reviewing the Story—1. twenty-six; 2. Carnegie Hall; 3. violin; 4. orchestra; 5. American Youth Orchestra; 6. conductor; 7. Symphonies at Midnight; 8. Award of Merit

PAGE 42
Finding the Meanings—1. special; 2. secret; 3. errand; 4. terrible; 5. privilege; 6. polite; 7. mistake; 8. attempt

PAGES 42 AND 43
Reviewing the Story—1. Betsey Bailey; 2. seven; 3. mother; 4. Baltimore, Mrs. Auld; 5. first, shipyard; 6. Bailey, Douglass; 7. England; 8. Maryland; 9. Anna Murray; 10. newspaper

PAGE 46
Reviewing the Story—1. blood plasma; 2. Morgan College; 3. transfusions; 4. McGill University; 5. baseball; 6. Washington, D.C.; 7. Columbia University; 8. John Beatie; 9. Howard University; 10. swimmer, four; 11. teacher

PAGE 47
Finding Homonyms—1. c; 2. f; 3. h; 4. e; 5. j; 6. a; 7. i; 8. b; 9. g; 10. d

PAGE 50
Finding the Meanings—*Meanings will vary. Suggested:* 1. a person who travels to little-known places; 2. an area of rolling land with grass but no trees; 3. a person who buys and sells things for a profit; 4. the farthest part of a settled country; 5. a person who attacks and robs ships
Understanding the Story—1. false; 2. true; 3. false; 4. true; 5. true; 6. false

PAGES 50 AND 51
Reviewing the Story—1. settlement; 2. pirate, merchant; 3. wrecked, hurricane; 4. Chicago; 5. St. Louis; 6. St. Louis, Montreal, Canada; 7. 1745, St. Marc, Haiti; 8. Paris, France; 9. Chicago Historical Society; 10. pioneers

PAGE 54
Reviewing the Story—1. b; 2. c; 3. c; 4. a; 5. b; 6. c
Finding Antonyms—1. death; 2. poor; 3. ashamed; 4. easier; 5. weakness; 6. never; 7. bold; 8. ended

PAGE 57
Reviewing the Story—1. b; 2. c; 3. a; 4. c; 5. b; 6. c; 7. b; 8. a
Finding Homonyms—1. e; 2. g; 3. c; 4. a; 5. f; 6. b; 7. h; 8. d

PAGES 59 AND 60
Reviewing the Story—1. Ambassador, Luxembourg; 2. Howard; 3. trial attorney, Justice; 4. Senate; 5. George Washington University; 6. International Business Machines; 7. law firm; 8. William Beasley Harris

PAGE 60
Finding Synonyms—*Synonyms will vary. Suggested:* 1. consequence; 2. hired; 3. beginning; 4. different; 5. talent; 6. superb; 7. remarkable; 8. impermanent

PAGE 63
Reviewing the Story—1. Amherst; 2. Harvard Law School; 3. taught; 4. black; 5. Howard University, Washington, D.C.; 6. government lawyer; 7. Osage; 8. Franklin D. Roosevelt
Finding Synonyms—1. stop; 2. take; 3. spare; 4. just; 5. significant; 6. finish; 7. choose; 8. rule; 9. unoccupied; 10. establish

PAGE 64
Understanding the Story—1. c; 2. f; 3. b; 4. e; 5. a; 6. d

PAGES 66 AND 67
Understanding the Story—1. Patrick Healey entered the Jesuit Novitiate in Maryland. 2. He taught at St. Joseph's College and at Holy Cross College. 3. It is in Belgium. 4. His father was an Irish planter. 5. He received it in 1865. 6. *Three of these four:* Father Healy improved the curriculum, reorganized the medical and law schools, organized an alumni association, and guided the construction of a building with administration, classroom, and dormitory facilities. 7. 1874, 1882. 8. He is buried in the campus graveyard at Georgetown University.

PAGE 67
Finding the Meanings—1. d; 2. f; 3. a; 4. g; 5. i; 6. b; 7. e; 8. h; 9. j; 10. c

PAGE 70
Finding Synonyms—1. e; 2. f; 3. a; 4. c; 5. h; 6. d; 7. b; 8. g

PAGES 70 AND 71
Reviewing the Story—1. b; 2. c; 3. b; 4. a; 5. c; 6. c; 7. c; 8. b; 9. c; 10. a

PAGE 71
Understanding the Story—1. true; 2. false; 3. true; 4. false; 5. false; 6. true; 7. true; 8. false
PAGE 74
Understanding the Story—1. e; 2. i; 3. j; 4. g; 5. c; 6. h; 7. b; 8. f; 9. d; 10. a
Reviewing the Story—1. c; 2. b; 3. b; 4. b
PAGE 75
Finding Synonyms—1. c; 2. h; 3. e; 4. a; 5. g; 6. j; 7. f; 8. i; 9. b; 10. d
PAGES 77 and 78
Understanding the Story—1. true; 2. false; 3. true; 4. true; 5. false; 6. false; 7. false; 8. true; 9. false; 10. true; 11. true; 12. false
PAGE 78
Finding Antonyms—1. weak; 2. poor; 3. lazy; 4. healthy 5. bored; 6. dark; 7. future; 8. peace
PAGES 80 AND 81
Understanding the Story—1. She studied law at Boston University. 2. *Three of these five:* She became the first black woman to be elected to Congress from the South, to serve in the Texas senate, to preside over a state senate, to serve as governor, and to serve on the Texas Legislative Council as a first-term senator. 3. She was selected as one of the top ten most influential women in Texas. 4. It is the House Judiciary Committee. 5. The prediction was made because of Barbara Jordan's dynamic work in politics. 6. She taught at Tuskegee Institute in Alabama.
PAGE 81
Finding the Meanings—1. g; 2. d; 3. h; 4. a; 5. i; 6. c; 7. b; 8. e; 9. j; 10. f
PAGE 83
Understanding the Story—1. true; 2. false; 3. false; 4. true; 5. false; 6. false; 7. false; 8. true; 9. true; 10. false; 11. true
PAGE 84
Finding Synonyms—1. e; 2. c; 3. g; 4. a; 5. h; 6. d; 7. b; 8. f
PAGE 87
Reviewing the Story—1. associate justice; 2. Supreme Court; 3. Howard University; 4. Baltimore; 5. N.A.A.C.P. and its Legal Defense and Educational Fund; 6. Topeka, Kansas; 7. segregation; 8. federal judge; 9. reverse; 10. solicitor general; 11. Supreme Court
PAGE 88
Finding Antonyms—1. biased; 2. innocent; 3. part; 4. higher; 5. failure; 6. slow; 7. beginning; 8. allow
PAGES 90 AND 91
Understanding the Story—1. true; 2. false; 3. false; 4. true; 5. false; 6. true; 7. false; 8. true; 9. false; 10. false
PAGE 91
Finding Antonyms—1. stay; 2. long; 3. inland; 4. lose; 5. bought; 6. easy; 7. import; 8. quick; 9. failure; 10. elderly
PAGE 95
Finding the Meanings—1. f; 2. d; 3. g; 4. b; 5. h; 6. c; 7. a; 8. e; 9. j; 10. i
PAGES 95 AND 96
Reviewing the Story—1. Joe DiMaggio; 2. outfielder; 3. pitcher, outfield; 4. Birmingham Black Barons; 5. high school; 6. New York Giants; 7. 1951; 8. home run; 9. 1954, 1965; 10. breadbasket; 11. New Jersey; 12. Say Hey
PAGE 98
Finding the Meanings—1. c; 2. e; 3. h; 4. f; 5. a; 6. d; 7. b; 8. g
PAGE 99
Understanding the Story—1. Constance Motley was born in New Haven, Connecticut. 2. A businessman, Clarence W. Blakeslee, helped to finance her education. 3. Constance Baker Motley played basketball and took part in debate. 4. He studied to become a lawyer. 5. She represented the state of New York. 6. The court case involving James Meredith was directed by Constance Motley. 7. She worked as a clerk for the N.A.A.C.P. Legal and Educational Defense Fund. 8. President Lyndon Johnson chose Constance Motley to be a United States district judge.
PAGE 102
Finding Antonyms—1. c; 2. f; 3. e; 4. a; 5. g; 6. h; 7. d; 8. b
PAGES 102 AND 103
Reviewing the Story—1. 200-meter dash; 2. James Cleveland, J.C.; 3. Ralph Metcalfe; 4. Berlin, Germany; 5. Buckeye Bullet; 6. ambassador of goodwill

PAGE 103
Understanding the Story—1. He won four gold medals. 2. He worked in a shoe shop. 3. He set the track record while in junior high school. 4. The government asked him to direct an athletic program for the armed forces. 5. He learned that success depends on fair play, hard work, and good standards.
PAGES 106 AND 107
Understanding the Story—1. *Three of these five:* Leontyne Price performed in the leading roles in *Antony and Cleopatra, Porgy and Bess, Tosca, Aïda,* and *Il Trovatore.* 2. They provided money for her while she was in college and when she received her scholarship in music. 3. Leontyne Price has never forgotten the people who helped her as she began her career. She is also busy in civic work. 4. She has received the Freedom Medal and the Italian Award of Merit. 5. Sometimes Mrs. Price did the music teacher's washing and ironing to pay for the music lessons. Mr. and Mrs. Price traded their Victrola as a down payment on a piano.
PAGE 107
Reviewing the Story—1. piano; 2. toy; 3. scholarship; 4. Chisholm; 5. Ira Gershwin; 6. William Warfield; 7. Freedom Medal; 8. United Negro College Fund
PAGE 108
Finding Synonyms—1. d; 2. g; 3. b; 4. f; 5. a; 6. h; 7. e; 8. c
PAGE 111
Reviewing the Story—1. three; 2. legs, walk; 3. basketball; 4. track, basketball; 5. ambassador of goodwill; 6. trophy, sportsmanship
Finding Homonyms—1. cent; 2. to or too; 3. new; 4. buy; 5. wood; 6. week; 7. their; 8. grate
PAGES 111 AND 112
Understanding the Story—1. She was named "Female Athlete of the Year." 2. Mrs. Rudolph believed that Wilma would walk again. Once a week Wilma and her mother traveled by bus to a hospital for special medical treatments for Wilma's leg. 3. The Olympic Games were held in Rome, Italy. 4. Wilma Rudolph overcame her handicap, set her goal, and worked toward that end. 5. Wilma Rudolph had scarlet fever and pneumonia as a child. The sickness affected one of her legs, and she was unable to walk.
PAGES 114 AND 115
Understanding the Story—1. Dr. Spurlock wanted to help relieve suffering and pain. 2. She received the degree from Howard University. 3. She completed the residency program at Cook County Psychopathic Hospital. 4. Dr. Spurlock served as attending psychiatrist. 5. Dr. Spurlock received the Strecker Award and the Professional Leadership Award. 6. Dr. Spurlock is deputy medical director. 7. Meharry Medical College is in Nashville, Tennessee. 8. Dr. Spurlock became chairperson of the department of psychiatry. 9. Dr. Spurlock was a member of major committees in her field, maintained various teaching positions, was chairperson of the department of psychiatry at Meharry Medical College, worked for the National Institute of Mental Health, became deputy medical director for the American Psychiatric Association, and joined the staffs of Howard University and George Washington University.
PAGE 115
Finding the Meanings—1. d; 2. f; 3. a; 4. h; 5. b; 6. g; 7. c; 8. e
PAGE 118
Reviewing the Story—1. b; 2. c; 3. a; 4. c; 5. c; 6. b; 7. b; 8. c; 9. b; 10. c; 11. a
PAGE 119
Finding the Meanings—*Meanings will vary. Suggested:* 1. honesty and sincerity; 2. people from whom one is descended; 3. to say no or decline to accept; 4. the first appearance of light in the morning; 5. to commit oneself to a certain course of action; 6. a person who emancipates a nation, people, etc.; 7. to freely offer one's services; 8. one or more persons making the rounds watching and guarding.
PAGE 122
Finding Synonyms—1. i; 2. e; 3. a; 4. f; 5. c; 6. j; 7. h; 8. d; 9. b; 10. g
Understanding the Story—1. true; 2. false; 3. false; 4. true; 5. false; 6. true; 7. false
PAGE 125
Finding Homonyms—1. c; 2. j; 3. h; 4. f; 5. a; 6. l; 7. i; 8. d; 9. g; 10. b; 11. k; 12. e
PAGES 125 AND 126
Reviewing the Story—1. b; 2. a; 3. c; 4. b; 5. c; 6. a; 7. c; 8. b; 9. a; 10. c; 11. c; 12. b